Margaret Mitchell

Twayne's United States Authors Series

Joseph M. Flora, Editor

University of North Carolina, Chapel Hill

TUSAS 566

Margaret Mitchell.
Photograph courtesy of the Bettman Archive.

Margaret Mitchell

By Elizabeth I. Hanson

Temple University

Twayne Publishers • Boston
A Division of G. K. Hall & Co.

Margaret Mitchell
Elizabeth I. Hanson

Copyright 1991 by G. K. Hall & Co.
All rights reserved.
Published by Twayne Publishers
A division of G. K. Hall & Co.
70 Lincoln Street
Boston, Massachusetts 02111

Copyediting supervised by Barbara Sutton.
Book production by Janet Z. Reynolds.
Book design by Barbara Anderson.
Typeset by Compset, Inc., Beverly, Massachusetts.

First published 1990.
10 9 8 7 6 5 4 3 2 1

Library of Congress Cataloging-in-Publication Data

Hanson, Elizabeth I.
    Margaret Mitchell / by Elizabeth I. Hanson.
        p.   cm.—(Twayne's United States authors series ; TUSAS 566)
    Includes bibliographical references and index.
    ISBN 0-8057-7608-7
    1. Mitchell, Margaret, 1900–1949.   2. Mitchell, Margaret,
1900–1949.   Gone with the wind.   3. Novelists, American—20th
century—Biography.   I. Title.   II. Series.
PS3525.I972Z68   1990
813'.52—dc20
    [B]   90-39258
                                                                                CIP

To William Hedges

Contents

About the Author

Elizabeth I. Hanson is a professor of American literature and writing at Temple University, Philadelphia. Her research interests are in the study of race and gender in American fiction. Her publications include books on the Native American in American literature and on race and gender in contemporary Native American fiction. She has also written the first critical biography of the Native American critic and poet Paulo Gunn Allen. She is currently at work on a critical study of Ellen Glasgow.

Preface

> If the novel *Gone with the Wind* has a theme, the theme is that of survival.
> —Margaret Mitchell[1]

Margaret Mitchell's masterwork, *Gone with the Wind* (1936), was designed to portray the perceptions, the growth, and the change necessary for survival. Mitchell was an American woman writer enfolded in paradoxes of success and of failure. She saw herself as a survivor and she succeeded in telling a remarkable tale of survival. That tale provides us with an intensely autobiographical portrait of a young woman entranced by ambition, power, and her own ability to attract men, yet confused by both that power and the men. Mitchell's fiction offers a vision of the complex, even perverse, ambiguities and contradictions inherent in women's experience in American literary culture.

Mitchell's single novel, *Gone with the Wind,* has survived even its own popularity. One critical commonplace of feminist interpretation is that the popularity of novels by women—whether Stowe's *Uncle Tom's Cabin,* Warner's *The Wide, Wide World,* or Mitchell's *Gone with the Wind*—has prevented them from receiving critical attention and has excluded them from the American literary canon. As the most popular of popular books, *Gone with the Wind* has, paradoxically, received the least attention, even from feminist critics. As unpopular among critics as it is popular among readers, *Gone with the Wind* deserves a carefully balanced and searching evaluation. To the exploration of Mitchell's work and life—the legends, the distortions, the caricature of her personality and the paradox of her popularity—this critical biography can now address itself.

The history of the American literary marketplace reveals a pattern of remarkable growth in sales of novels, beginning in the 1850s; for example, in 1830 a sale of 6,500 copies of a novel would have been registered as a commercial success; yet by 1852 Stowe's *Uncle Tom's Cabin* achieved a sale of more than 300,000 copies.[2] What propelled book buyer market forces during this period and what propels them still in the 1990s are the effects of democratization and feminization within American culture. Popular books, especially immensely popular books—ones that sell in the numbers recorded by *Uncle Tom's Cabin* or *Gone with the Wind*—are purchased by both male and female readers, of course. What is so interesting about the success of Stowe and Mitchell is that their books do *not* assume an audience of only men or only women, although in both Stowe's and Mitchell's cases, the focus of their fiction is on the survival of the vulnerable, whether black or female.

Each of these works also explores the tensions inherent in a time in American history when masculine and aristocratic values and powers were being modified by rapid increases in the American population, by growing industrialization and urbanization, especially in the North, by the development of a range of social reform efforts, including anti-slavery and women's movements, by the spread of free public education, and by political pressures, particularly in western states' demands to share power and wealth.[3] Amid these conflicts, the Civil War was inevitable. What Stowe did was to attack a major concern of the 1850s, slavery, and her novel sold in the millions, kept printing presses running night and day, and generated an adoring reading public. What Mitchell did was to attack a major concern of the 1930s, economic survival, and her novel sold in the millions, kept printing presses running day and night, and generated an adoring reading public. *Uncle Tom's Cabin* ministered to the psychic needs of the antebellum world while predicting the inevitable resolution of the era's tensions in civil war, and *Gone with the Wind* tended to the ambiguities and confusions of the postbellum world that remained unresolved despite the Civil War. Neither Stowe nor Mitchell, amazingly enough, offered political programs, compelled violent revolutions, or suggested radical reforms. Instead, each trusted in the American individual's capacity to transform a world in crisis. Both located their greatest trust in women's potential for transformative action, just as both held men responsible for the disasters women would seek to correct. Both Stowe and Mitchell would be accused of naive oversimplifications, but it may well have been Stowe's belief that "there is one thing that every individual can do—they can see to it that *they feel right*" and Mitchell's belief that a woman "could stand it." As individuals, they too could "feel right" and they too could "stand anything." Stowe's and Mitchell's visions of American selfhood became part of the universally shared and sharable American experience.

Given the subject matter of each of these best-sellers by women, their success in the marketplace was not surprising. The wide scale of the canvas on which these portraits of the American South were painted and the extraordinary range of emotion the authors explore make them more than texts; they became events in the lives of readers, events so powerfully felt that they had to be shared within communities of readers for their full impact to emerge. Sales figures for *Uncle Tom's Cabin* and *Gone with the Wind* indicated a geometric rise in book purchases as readers informed other readers on a massive scale. No reviewer could stimulate or control such sales, just as no critic can penetrate the inexhaustible sensibility that determines the American reader's response to such literary experiences.

Certainly, Margaret Mitchell found it difficult to comprehend her own success. She spent much of the last decade and a half of her life seeking to survive her own triumph and choosing quite deliberately to avoid writing any additional literary triumphs for the market place. But if she found the effect of her novel difficult to understand, her confusion was completely superseded by that of literary critics for the past half century, who have found a good deal more to praise and interpret in *Uncle Tom's Cabin* than in *Gone with the Wind*.[4]

Given this curious critical response to Mitchell's triumphant tale, it is, above all, necessary to dispel the belief that there is no literary art, no serious significance, in *Gone with the Wind*. It is true that the book was written by a woman; it is true that the book has sold millions of copies; and it is true that the book is largely preoccupied with feminine responses to disaster, but these are not sufficient reasons for exclusion from the American literary canon. Indeed, these are the precise reasons for a new evaluation of Mitchell's work within the canon. Or for a new means of evaluating the canon itself.

If there is an art to *Gone with the Wind*, what of the person who devised it so copiously, so passionately? Is it true that Mitchell herself, like her heroine, "never understood either of the men she had loved and so she had lost them both"?[5] How could a woman produce such a literary phenomenon as *Gone with the Wind*, having lived so inconspicuous and unliterary a life? Did nothing happen to Margaret Mitchell except the writing of a single work of fiction? Is the popularity of her book held against her by literary critics so much that they fail to explore how the text affects large numbers of readers?

These are the guiding questions of this critical study of Mitchell and her novel. Although no critic can write or explain precisely what a literary artist may have written out of his or her own experience, the critic can attempt to comprehend and describe what went on in Mitchell's creation of self and in the articulation of that self, at one remove, in her art. A creative personality such as Mitchell's is rare, for she has created a work of fiction that has connected with the emotions and responses of a large mass audience both in America and abroad for more than half a century.

What is unique to Mitchell is the voice of Scarlett, bold and sassy as Atlanta itself. Scarlett is believable because she speaks of an authentic self and a credible, if complex, personality. Here is a real person who assumes risks, who allows the energy and significance of her Tara to possess her, and who testifies to the value of hard-won survival. In this critical study of Mitchell and her *Gone with the Wind*, I will show a literary artist who was anything but blind to the shortcomings of the simple response, but nonetheless was capable of offering simple answers to hard questions. Yet, always she sought to reveal the range of ambiguities, complexities, and corruptions in the culture and characters of *Gone with the Wind*. Mitchell's Scarlett and the world of manmade disaster she inhabits also contain a prophetic vision of modern man and woman seeking to accommodate themselves to each other and to circumstance.

The great balancing formulas of *Gone with the Wind* are never resolved. Instead, Mitchell provided her readers with the capacity to see, to know, and to feel the possibilities of resolution of the conflict between Scarlett and Rhett—indeed, the confrontations inevitable to passionate men and women who are striving for themselves. The text of *Gone with the Wind* is a point of departure for its readers' imaginations. In this book I will explore how Mitchell employs her own imaginative family history as well as the real facts of her experience as a southern belle, Smith College freshman, and newspaper reporter to devise the elements that so captivated her readers. Although this study is more than a biography, the autobiographical significance of *Gone with the Wind* demands that I begin with Mitchell's own life, especially in relation to her parents' and grandparents' generations. From that foundation, Mitchell built her novel. *Gone with the Wind* was not written in isolation, and in addition to Mitchell's family influences, she was inspired by the dimensions of literary modernism in the 1920s and 1930s. And she was amused and appalled by the development of her novel into an extraordinary American film. All these elements of Mitchell's biography and the evolution of her text demand our attention and promise to repay our efforts, for we have seen nothing quite like *Gone with the Wind*.

Elizabeth I. Hanson

Temple University

Acknowledgments

It is always a pleasure to give thanks, and in the writing of *Margaret Mitchell* thanksgivings are a particular source of joy because many generous friends and colleagues have offered encouragement and assistance along the way. I thank Professor Kenneth Eble for initiating the project, Professor Joseph Flora for editing the book with care and speed, Elizabeth Fowler for managing the project with kindness and understanding, Hilary Polk and Barbara Sutton for their skill in copyediting, Janet Reynolds for the efficient production of the book, and J. Robert Cockrell, M.D. for his never-failing concern. I thank Professor William Hedges for his warmth and friendship, Brandt and Brandt for permission to quote from *Margaret Mitchell of Atlanta,* the William Morris Agency for permission to quote from *Gone with the Wind,* Mr. George Brightbill of the Temple University Urban Archives for his understanding and assistance, and, as always, my parents and my brother, Luther, for the love and trust they bestow so faithfully.

Chronology

1900   Margaret Mitchell born 8 November in Atlanta, Georgia, the second child of Eugene and Maybelle (Stephens) Mitchell.

1914   Completes elementary school in the Atlanta Public School system and enters Washington Seminary in Atlanta.

1918   Enters Smith College (Northampton, Mass.) and becomes engaged to marry Clifford Henry. Henry dies from wounds suffered during World War I in France on 16 October.

1919   Mother dies 25 January in the influenza epidemic. Mitchell withdraws from Smith College after completing her freshman year to care for her father and brother in Atlanta.

1922   Marries Berrien K. ("Red") Upshaw 1 September. John R. Marsh serves as best man at the wedding. By November, Upshaw physically abuses and deserts Mitchell. In December Mitchell seeks and gains a position as feature writer on the *Atlanta Journal Sunday Magazine.*

1925   Divorced from Upshaw, marries John Marsh 4 July.

1926   Quits her job with the *Sunday Magazine* and begins doing research in Civil War history.

1929   Completes the manuscript of her Civil War historical novel and sets it aside.

1935   Harold Latham, an executive of Macmillan Publishing Co., meets Mitchell and persuades her to let him consider the dilapidated text of what would become *Gone with the Wind.* He accepts the novel for publication and sends her a contract on 17 July.

1936   *Gone with the Wind* published on 30 June.

1937   *Gone with the Wind* wins Pulitzer Prize.

1939   Mitchell receives M.A. from Smith College. David Selznick's film version of *Gone with the Wind* premieres in Atlanta 15 December.

1949   Mitchell dies 16 December of injuries suffered in an automobile accident in Atlanta.

Chapter One
A Child of Atlanta

"They burned you," she thought, "and they laid you flat. But they didn't lick you. They couldn't lick you. You'll grow back just as big and sassy as you used to be!" (*GW*, 555)

Margaret Mitchell, above all else, was a child of Atlanta. Her attachments to her native city were complex and varied, at times even frustrating, but they remained singularly close and affecting. The Mitchell-Stephens family, like the city of Margaret Mitchell's birth, was a curious amalgam of diverse elements all of which interacted to ensure outer success, although the stresses and strains of the assemblage lurked within to test and disturb. The Civil War caused the dismantling of many old, powerful orders and hierarchies in the South. The freeing of enslaved blacks was only one kind of southern social liberation; many relatively poor whites derived economic and social worth in newly urbanized and industrialized centers such as Atlanta. The Mitchell-Stephens clan was forged out of this white reordering of the southern economic landscape; and doubtless Margaret Mitchell's own passion for discovering the meaning of that restructuring—what is defined as Reconstruction—stemmed from her own family's highly successful, yet deeply stressful family experience in the postbellum American South.

Margaret Mitchell was to make her own success out of that family experience. But it was the successful enterprise of her father and brother, especially in law and real estate (two allied professional activities that were closely connected with the development of the city of Atlanta over the last century), that so compelled the energy of the Mitchell-Stephens family. The family enterprise was largely a male-dominated one, but not wholly so. When Eugene Mitchell chose Maybelle Stephens for his wife, he was deliberately and knowingly selecting a woman of high intelligence and strong opinions concerning women's education and their right to full participation not merely in family decisions but in political decisions. In fact, his wife became an ardent suffragist. Both Eugene Mitchell and Maybelle Stephens demanded substantial commitments of support from one another, just as they expressed high expectations of success from their two children, Stephens and Margaret. Both children fulfilled those demands and kept those commitments.

The major portion of the Mitchell-Stephens family hope for future success devolved, as it normally does in families, on their firstborn son, significantly named Stephens Mitchell (b. 1895). It would be Stephens Mitchell who would seek to protect and enhance the family energies, creative and economic, for the rest of his life. It would be Stephens Mitchell, not Margaret Mitchell, who would record the family version of its own history. His autobiographical portrait of the Mitchell-Stephens clan has as its dominant theme not survival, the theme Margaret Mitchell defines for her creative history, but serenity: "Probably the only remarkable thing about Margaret's childhood was that it was so unremarkable. It was serene and happy in a way that was possible only in a world where one felt absolutely secure."[1] Stephens Mitchell's memory was, however, strikingly at variance with the realities of postbellum Atlanta.

The world of Eugene Mitchell and Maybelle Stephens in Reconstruction Atlanta and particularly in the Jackson Hill section where they each grew up was very far from serene or secure. Both of Mitchell's parents were born in the period immediately following the war— Eugene Mitchell in 1866 and Maybelle Stephens in 1872—and their lives and the lives of their children were deeply and fundamentally influenced by the effects of the war and particularly of the Union government's policies toward Georgia. For example, Margaret Mitchell herself remembered this period through the eyes of her own parents, even though they themselves had not been born during the war and had virtually no memory of the period during which the Reconstruction Acts of Congress had ruled Georgia from Washington, D.C. She wrote, "I heard so much about the fighting and the hard times after the war that I firmly believed Mother and Father had been through it all instead of being born long afterward. In fact I was about ten years old before I learned the war hadn't ended shortly before I was born."[2] Here Mitchell made an extraordinarily revealing identification with the experience of her own parents, for *they* had been the ones who had been born shortly after the war had ended. It was the experience of Mitchell's parents that formed and informed Mitchell's own perception of the meaning of the Civil War, and it was through their efforts to cope with the climate of disruption into which they were born that Mitchell designed the world of Scarlett O'Hara and Rhett Butler.

Following the Civil War, social conflict between blacks and whites and between poor whites and less poor whites (few even somewhat well-off white southerners existed in Georgia after the war because most of their capital had been invested in slaves, who were no longer their or anyone's property) corroded and disrupted efforts to rebuild Atlanta. The old order was in disarray, and a new order was in embryo. Civil strife within Georgia politics was reflected in the continuing drama of constitutional conventions imposed, deposed, and then reimposed by federal fiat. The effects of so many constitutional conventions, each with their own forms of constitutional governments (constitutions were composed in 1861, 1865, 1867, and 1877), were constant challenge and disorientation within a nearly chaotic political system. Planter dominance of the Georgia civil government was attacked not merely by the federal government in Washington, but by newly freed blacks, nearly starving yeomen farmers, and desperate businessmen, all of whom sought to revive the Georgian economy and to blame the old planter leadership for their financial woes.[3]

The Civil War had brought economic disaster to Georgia that did not dissipate with the end of the conflict. In 1860, a free adult white male Georgian owned property worth about $4,000, approximately twice the estate possessed by the average nonsouthern, white man. By 1870, the time of Mitchell's parents' birth, the average wealth of all Georgia men—white and black—was approximately $1,000, less than half the nonsouthern average.[4] Poor harvests in the late 1860s, the virtually total lack of capital in the state—newly emancipated slaves had absorbed much of Georgia's investment income, for Georgians had owned well over $400 million in slave property—and the collapse of Confederate currency made Georgia fundamentally vulnerable to the interests of bankers, lawyers, industrialists, merchants, and real estate brokers who understood their own advantages and were capable of exploiting the weak, depressed, and undermined economy of the state.[5]

Powerful figures—some southern and some northern—amassed substantial wealth rapidly and with ease. Their formulas for success would be represented by the reality principle of Rhett Butler in *Gone with the Wind*. Amid defeated and demoralized planters, a new power elite would assume control of Atlanta and of Georgia without firing a shot. What the North had required years of battle to accomplish, the successful businessmen of Atlanta achieved without violence and, what proved even more striking perhaps, with respectability.

The ideological conflicts that so devastated southern experience amid the disestablishment of the old planter hierarchical order were exacerbated by economic pressures and civil disorder in the decades following the war. The old creeds, which justified, indeed glorified, the plantation ideal, had been thrown asunder by the Emancipation Proclamation of 1863, just as the economic worth of the planter elite had been rendered bankrupt. The need for an ideological defense of southern values remained, however, and a new formulation was created from the literal and metaphorical ashes of Atlanta's experience in the summer of 1864. The burning of the city and the failure to defend its civilians were fashioned into an ideological justification for failure. The loss of Atlanta's power and wealth as a city became the Lost Cause. The mythic foundation of a Lost Cause was grounded in the social, political, and economic failures of southerners as a whole.[6] If theirs was a Lost Cause, how could they ever have succeeded? And, more proximately, how could they ever succeed again?

Some southerners barely survived the Civil War and its aftermath, and some southerners actually prospered amid disaster, but the Lost Cause held them all to its canons of faith. The mythology of the Lost Cause encompassed a range of mutually reinforcing ideological positions based on the essential benevolence of white southerners toward blacks, the righteousness of the South's actions during the Civil War, the courage of southern white males, the sacrifices of southern white females, and the loyalty of southern blacks. Such an ideology is profoundly conservative; its reason for being is to reassure and secure those who believe. The code of the Lost Cause legitimized failure and, ultimately, made respectable the overly aggressive new power structure that came to rule Atlanta in the decades following the war.

This new economic elite was formed during the period of relatively fluid culture in Atlanta right after the war by a combination of factors: the death or financial ruin of the old planter elite in the war, the escalation in property values in Atlanta after it became the capital of the state during the constitutional convention of 1867 (the convention assembled in Atlanta because Milledgeville, the former capital, refused to accommodate black delegates, and so the convention voted to move the new capital), and the development of the city as a major railroad terminus and manufacturing site. One systematic study of Atlanta's wealthy and powerful found a group of new men who persistently made their way not through planter connections or through inheritance—the traditional source of wealth and power—but through education, effort, and merit.[7] One such man was Margaret Mitchell's father, Eugene Mitchell, a southerner without planter pretensions and with a compulsion to succeed.

The Atlanta elite in the postbellum period was composed of talented southern natives—carpetbaggers were not welcome in this rarefied company—with aggressive, although fundamentally conservative values. Change was inevitable in this city whose upper-class members, neighborhoods, and means of wealth had been devastated; those who replaced the old elite in the new socially and economically mobile Atlanta were also concerned with social and economic stability. The goal of the old and new elites was the same: order. The new blood, like the old, was transfused through a system intent on survival and obsessed with respectability.

In this intellectual, social, and economic atmosphere the Mitchell-Stephens family sought to find its own power and its own respectability. Indeed, Margaret Mitchell's father had desired to be a writer himself but was compelled by his father and by economic circumstances to find a more "honorable" position in Atlanta society as a lawyer and real estate expert. With support from his father and his brother, Gordon, Eugene Mitchell studied law at the University of Georgia and joined his brother in law practice in Atlanta. In the early 1890s, Eugene Mitchell began his shrewd real estate investments, based in part on his legal knowledge of various businesses in Atlanta, and he also sought to court the petite and well-educated Maybelle Stephens. Both pursuits reflected Eugene Mitchell's carefully planned entry into Atlanta's economic elite. Many Atlantans built or augmented their wealth by investing heavily in real estate in a city where property values escalated at an amazing pace. Marriage to Maybelle Stephens, a daughter of Annie Fitzgerald Stephens, connected Eugene Mitchell to the old planter elite of Georgia, for Maybelle was descended from the Fitzgeralds who had owned a plantation of 2,375 acres and thirty-five slaves before much of it had been destroyed and lost in the Civil War.[8] In love and in business, Eugene Mitchell succeeded in making his own way on his own terms.

The path he chose led him quickly and directly to the elite of Atlanta. Eugene Mitchell rose rapidly to a position of civic leadership, and by 1911 he was president of the Atlanta Bar Association and a leading member of the Atlanta Board of Education. As a patent and real estate attorney, Mitchell was devoted to protecting the patent rights and real estate transactions of his fellow successful businessmen, mainly merchants and industrialists, who were themselves building the new Atlanta. Mitchell rose with their tide, and they were clearly grateful for the protection he offered and the security he sought for them and for himself as well.

The reason Eugene Mitchell was so compulsively desirous of security was that he had lost a substantial investment in the Panic of 1893, early in his marriage to Maybelle Stephens. For decades thereafter, both of Margaret Mitchell's parents considered themselves financially threatened and were consumed with anxiety about their own affluence. No other community in Georgia could compare with Atlanta in the rapid pace of its economic development or in the aggressive social leadership of its elite. Inevitably, the more that elite gained, the more it could not stand to lose. Affluent city-dwellers like the Mitchells, who purchased a highly visible mansion on Peachtree Street in August 1912, were concerned by the social turmoil and high crime rates that accompanied so much growth. It was no accident that in 1913 Atlanta became the first city in Georgia to enact an ordinance promoting racial segregation within city residential blocks such as those in the fashionable Peachtree Street vicinity. Pressed and concerned by the problems created by the urban growth they themselves had created, the Atlanta elite became increasingly reformist concerning social policy to protect their economic and social interests. Paradoxically, reformism and conservatism were the interrelated ideologies chosen to defend Atlanta's new urban development. But any programs of reform served to reinforce subtly the essential conservatism of the culture, whether its leaders were the old planters or the new entrepreneurs who had taken their places and married their descendants.[9]

Eugene Mitchell and Maybelle Stephens's experience fit within the pattern of Atlanta elite marriages, and in many respects their experience shaped Margaret Mitchell's own view of the family constellation. In his book *Community Power Structure: A Study of Decision Makers* (1953) and its sequel, *Community Power Succession: Atlanta's Policy-Makers Revisited* (1980), Floyd Hunter studied the essential ethos of the Atlanta power structure in great detail from a sociological perspective. Margaret Mitchell explored the same families and the same patterns of succession from an aesthetic viewpoint in *Gone with the Wind*. The quest for success that so compelled Scarlett and Rhett Butler was repeated again and again in the data of family history and close observation collected by Hunter. Success based on a will to survive underlay the Atlanta miracle.

That miracle of development was bought with the coinage of effort, ability, and also a good deal of anxiety. When the elite of Atlanta built handsome new mansions, they also created segregation covenants to assure the value of their properties. Eugene Mitchell was so concerned about the security of his daughter Margaret in the Atlanta public schools that, even though he was a member of the School Board, he removed her from the local public school and enrolled her in the Washington Seminary. Later, both Stephens Mitchell and Margaret Mitchell were sent north to complete their education in schools that offered greater prestige and enhanced security—Stephens attended Harvard Law School and Margaret studied at Smith College. The cachet of a northern education followed by a return south was particularly important to Eugene and Maybelle Mitchell, and both encouraged and supported their children's education in northern academic institutions. Eugene Mitchell had graduated from the University of Georgia with honors in 1885 and had taken his law degree there in 1886. Maybelle Stephens had been educated at both the Bellevue Convent in Quebec and at the Atlanta Female Institute. For Eugene and Maybelle Mitchell, the education of their children was of primary importance not simply for the intrinsic values of learning for its own sake, but as an expression of the family's upper-middle-class caste and prominence in Atlanta society. Stephens Mitchell's Harvard law degrees separated him from those lawyers in Atlanta who, like his father, had trained at the University of Georgia Law School. Margaret Mitchell's experience at Smith College was also a source of distinction from other young Georgia women who generally completed their education at a seminary or institute, like Maybelle Stephens, or who might attend a southern women's college such as Agnes Scott in Decatur, Georgia. Assuming their children's success demanded that they follow a social and educational path different from their own, Eugene and Maybelle insisted that their children be distinguished from the experience of their peers in Atlanta.

The cost, both financial and emotional, of such a differentiation was carried by all the members of the family, as each was compelled to meet the challenge of adapting to cultural distinctions outside Atlanta and of meeting the demands of the culture within Atlanta upon return. For Stephens Mitchell, the tensions inherent in his parents' admonitions to succeed were muted by his quite easily gained success on his return to his native city. Following service in World War I, he joined his father's law firm, and, quite literally, replicated his father's life in his work, family, and household. For Margaret Mitchell, the demand to succeed was just as clearly expressed as it had been to her brother but to find a measure of that success and stability Stephens had accumulated so rapidly would prove much more difficult. Margaret sought to define her own success on her own terms.

Why was success and security so crucial to the Mitchell family? How could a young girl find her way toward this goal? Would she be able to resist her parents' demands on her? Or would she find her means of success through a form of literary domesticity of her own design? Margaret Mitchell was very strongly influenced by her parents' and brother's conceptions of themselves and their place in the world. When she undermined their view of her worth, particularly by her first disastrous marriage, however, she found that she became even more insistently the person her family sought to create. Her brother wrote in his autobiographical fragment, "We know a good deal about our forebears, and when I stop and think about them, and I think about Margaret, I believe I can see how each of the personalities behind us made its own contribution to her sum-total. Though we owed most, of course, to the characters of our parents, and their influence on us, behind them lay those others who formed us."[10] In Stephens's own terms, Margaret is the "sum-total" of a family equation. Her parents and her ancestors "formed" her to their own design; Margaret represented a mixture of the personalities and influences of other people, not actually a person except as she related to these other significant family figures, according to Stephens.

What was so interesting about Stephens's formulation of his sister's net worth was that he shaped her inner nature in *his* terms. His terms reflect those of his father, especially, but of his mother also. Stephens, born five years before Margaret, was an elder, stronger, highly significant figure in the family constellation, particularly to his much loved, petite sister with the fragile health and strong temper. He wished to see her and, above all, represent her as a being made by and within a family with a passion for security and inner assuredness. For example, Stephens remembered in his unpublished memoir his father's response to the Panic of 1893: the newly married Eugene and Maybelle had sustained significant losses, which had "taken out of him all daring and put in its place a desire to have a competence assured to him."[11]

Much more even than financial conservatism was expressed in this memory of family disaster; Eugene and Maybelle Mitchell felt their newly made family to be deeply shaken. In response, they continued to live in the home of Maybelle's mother, where they had first moved after their marriage in 1892, for a decade after the Panic. Finally, in 1902, when the family consisted of Maybelle and Eugene, a seven-year-old Stephens, and a two-year-old Margaret, they moved to a home owned by Annie Stephens. Still, the family security was assured by the generosity of Maybelle's mother. Eugene Mitchell's law practice prospered, and he husbanded his reserves with the assured competence his son has described, so that by 1903, after being married for more than eleven years and fathering two children, Eugene Mitchell purchased a home of his own for his own family. That home, where the family was to live for nearly a decade more, was located at 187 Jackson Street, not even a block away from Annie Stephens. For twenty years Eugene and Maybelle Mitchell lived on or near the family doorstep of Annie Stephens, and Stephens, their only son, spent his entire childhood and youth there until he entered the University of Georgia. It was not surprising that Stephens perceived his sister as just as inextricably interpenetrated by the family influence and security as he himself was, or that he thought of her as the "sum-total" of that generous, secure, yet total—the word itself is meaningful—family order.

Stephens was conscious of his family's powerful place in his own life and in the life of Atlanta: "It has always been a satisfaction," he wrote in his memoir, to know that "ours was one of the families that could refer to parents, grandparents, and great-grandparents who had lived in or near the city without embarrassment—in fact with pride."[12] He felt his own place in Atlanta was secured—as, indeed, it was—by those ancestors from whom he gained both financial and professional assurance. But for his sister, satisfaction in her ancestors would be an ambiguous and, at times, ironic experience. She wrote much later concerning southern expressions that the phrase "old and prominent" invariably preceded the word "family" no matter what the actual members of that family might achieve or fail to achieve.

For Margaret Mitchell, family came to signify a parental, and also grandparental, game of pull and tug. On the one hand, she was propelled, like her brother, into fulfilling the family's ideas of success and satisfaction through its "old and prominent" past to a new and prominent future, and, on the other hand, she was frequently controlled and

admonished, unlike her brother, for not accepting the deeper demands
and meanings implicit in "family," that is, for not being a conventional
"belle," for not marrying early and well, and for not producing heirs.
Her life and her writing of *Gone with the Wind* were to become the
means by which she engaged in a long search to comprehend the ambiguities of her origins.

Although essentially a very active and attractive child, Margaret
Mitchell was prone to serious, even life-threatening accidents and
learned from the age of three, when her first serious accident occurred,
that there were important advantages to be gained by a state of dependency in a family of aggressive personalities. Margaret possessed a family of two normal parents, an older brother who acted toward her in
the manner of a nearly parental figure, and a highly demanding and
critical grandmother. When, for example, she was nearly killed in a
fire as she stood over an open heating grate from which an overactive
draft forced flames up from the basement, Margaret was saved by
her mother, who wrapped her in blankets and rushed her to the hospital. During the long period of recuperation, Margaret received dot-
ing attention from all her elders. In a world that threatened and
controlled little girls, a paradoxical form of security might be found
through risk itself, for the aftermath of danger was devoted attention.
By accident and illness, Margaret, the weakest and smallest of
the Mitchell-Stephens family, became the one who dominated them
all. For the rest of her life, Mitchell's health and well-being continued
to be threatened by constant accidents and illnesses, and she died in
a car accident in 1949. She would never choose the path of safety
and caution; if some alternative danger was available, Mitchell would
grasp it.

But when the risk had subsided—indeed, amid the actual threat—
Mitchell turned immediately to her many parental figures, including
her second husband, John Marsh, who always assumed a fatherly role
with his wife. This lifelong pattern in which Mitchell searched for
hazards to her safety and then swiftly retreated to a security where she
was protected and allowed to dominate is explored in *Gone with the
Wind*. Threatening situations recur in the violent cycles of Scarlett's
experience, and at all times she is the central figure near disaster. Scarlett is obsessed by survival, but she never quite apprehends what occurs
around her. She is threatened, and she seeks security. Between these
absolute extremes—fear of loss and worship of security—the survival
theme of *Gone with the Wind* plays itself out in striking fashion. And,

usually, love from men threatens also. Men exact costs, unqualified devotion and sexual responsiveness, which are themselves threatening to Scarlett's survival-seeking identity. Women signify little in the equation, for they are passive, long-suffering, unperceptive, and remote from reality, like Scarlett's sisters. Only men and quasi-mother figures like Ellen and Melanie might offer some semblance of security, but they cannot be counted on to provide it. After all, motherly women die, and men seem actually to seek danger rather than to protect women from its risks.

In Mitchell's vision of Scarlett, she observed and portrayed her own improvisations on the theme of a woman's survival. In the artist's imagination one thing was certain: the imaginer controlled and dominated, and the rest of the world listened and appreciated. Mitchell chose the role of storyteller from the earliest age, and while recovering from her first serious accident, she listened to her grandmother's stories and told her own tales to the family that gathered around her bed. Her brother recorded that later "Margaret told stories and wrote them, and wrote and produced her own plays with the children around."[13] She remained a storyteller for the rest of her life.

Storytelling proved one path of safety, but it might be undermined by new threats of disaster, both actual and imagined. Mitchell's mother provided an ambivalent presence in her daughter's life; on the one hand, it was Maybelle who saved her life in the fire and cared for her as she recovered, and, on the other hand, it was Maybelle who insisted that the little girl attend school not simply as an exercise in education but as a means of survival. Thirty years after attending school for the first time, Mitchell recalled her mother's determination in a letter to the historian Henry Steele Commager. Maybelle had taken Margaret on a tour of the remains of devastated Atlanta in 1906 and "talked about the world those people had lived in" before the war. Margaret recorded that her mother had described "such a secure world, and how it had exploded beneath them. And she told me that my own world was going to explode under me, some day, and God help me if I didn't have some weapon to meet the new world. 'So for God's sake go to school and learn something that will stay with you. The strength of women's hands isn't worth anything but what they've got in their heads will carry them as far as they need to go.'" Mitchell described her reaction to this advice as "frightened and impressed," so much so that she learned to write well enough to gain a job on a newspaper when her first marriage ended in disaster.[14] Throughout her tutelage of her daughter, Maybelle Stephens sought to frighten and to impress, alternately to stifle and to encourage. Through her mother's efforts, Margaret learned that she might derive strength and support from her family and that, conversely, the family might deprive her of strength and support by frightening her through her own sense of dependency and through their own sense of dominance. How should she cope with a "frightening" and "impressing" family universe? What happens to anyone who seeks her own way? Without a mother to frighten and impress her, what path should she take?

Foremost among the appeals and considerations of Mitchell's childhood was her struggle in a family of competing and demanding egos to find her own identity. For Margaret, life in the Mitchell family was a state of rising expectations, as the family sought to transform itself beyond its Jackson Hill origins and middle-class status and, especially, its dependence on her grandmother, Annie Stephens. Eugene Mitchell approached the future breaking up of the longtime financial and personal connection to his mother-in-law with typical caution. In 1909 he purchased a lot on Peachtree Street, about a mile north of Ponce De Leon Avenue and three miles from the central business district of Atlanta at that time. The property was vacant for several years, but in August 1912, just before the beginning of a new school year for Margaret, the family moved to a newly completed home in the classical revival style. The home was actually designed as a mansion, for the ground floor of 1149 Peachtree Street covered seventy feet, complete with extensive carving, grand staircase, and high ceilings. Margaret finished the last two grades of her elementary education at the Tenth Street School, the local public school, and now lived at a considerable distance from her old friends and old life in Jackson Hill. Her father was deeply involved in his law practice—after all, he had considerable expense connected with the new house. Her mother had a much larger domestic staff to direct and new social demands on her time, and her brother had moved on to college. Margaret sought her own distractions and sought also to command some of the attention of the family. She wrote plays to be performed in the enormous new house, using the sitting room as a stage and the hall and music room opposite for the audience, and she rode her brother's horse, Bucephalus, a huge animal with a fast gallop, to escape the family's oppressive new social demands on their young and lovely daughter.[15]

At the turn of the century, daughters of upper-middle-class families entered women's seminaries and colleges in large numbers, and by the

1920s, prominent families expected their daughters, as well as their sons, to attend college and to reflect to the world outside the rising status and prestige of their origins. For Margaret, this expectation was defined for her by 1912. The Mitchell family determination to succeed, to reform, to modernize itself and their offspring was much in the spirit of American Progressivism, and locally dominant elites of Atlanta, in which Eugene and Maybelle Mitchell were numbered, mirrored the goals of Progressivism in Atlantan terms. The aims of southern progressives were complex, seemingly perversely ambiguous; nonetheless, they emanated from a range of sources, and they expressed deeply felt needs.

Chief among those needs was a conservative quest for security and stability in the social order of Atlanta. Progressivism evolved in Georgia following the Civil War and the social conflict, civil strife, and ideological dissension that consistently disrupted the social order of Georgia in the second half of the nineteenth century and the first decades of the twentieth.[16] The leaders of progressive reform movements were citizens like Eugene and Maybelle Mitchell who became involved in school boards, bar associations, women's suffrage activities, and so on, as a means of defining and supporting a clearly delineated social order based on success, merit, personal propriety, and individual responsibility. Poll taxes, white primaries, and literacy requirements ensured that virtually no blacks and few lower-income whites would disrupt the orderly political process or disturb the stable social order of Georgian society. Governor Hoke Smith, the state's most prominent Progressive leader, voiced the Atlantan concept of white responsibility and white superiority that pervades Margaret Mitchell's vision. He wrote in 1906, "Kindly, but firmly, the large majority of the negroes must be supervised and directed by the white man."[17] Amid the crises of continual social conflict and economic disaster, it is not surprising that leading citizens and governmental leaders would seek goals of order, stability, and the restoration of confidence. Eugene Mitchell, like Governor Smith, had sought to make a career in Atlanta where the legal profession was crowded and highly competitive. Mitchell succeeded in establishing himself despite obstacles, panics, and crises; he refused to relinquish the power he had gained to anyone but his own heirs. To Stephens and Margaret, his goals and his ideals would devolve.

Both of Margaret Mitchell's parents were reformist in the sense that they supported improved public education (although they did not hes-

itate to educate their own children in private institutions), woman's
suffrage, and similar measures. Maybelle Mitchell joined other members of the Atlanta elite in an effort to reassert upper-class stewardship
of the city's populace through charitable work and women's clubs. Like
many reformists, the Mitchells both distrusted politics and politi-
cians and sought social correctives through citizens' groups and, in
Maybelle's case, through hortatory lectures to rural women's groups.
Margaret Mitchell recalled several decades after her mother's death that
her "earliest memories were of my mother and the woman's suffrage
movement. Mother was small and gentle but redheaded, and nothing
infuriated her as much as the complacent attitude of other ladies who
felt that they should let the gentlemen do the voting. Our family was
fortunate in that the menfolks were heartily in favor of woman's suffrage."[18] While Maybelle Mitchell assumed a highly public role in special reform efforts, her husband continued to offer quiet but no less
significant leadership of citizens' groups. The Mitchell family based
their arguments for social reform on legal, economic, and practical
grounds; for example, Maybelle, like her mother and her mother's
many sisters, had inherited property, and she objected to paying taxes
without the privilege of voting. Whatever the family's commitment to
social reform, traditional views of women's responsibilities and wom-
en's role in society nevertheless exerted considerable influence in the
maturation of a young girl in the Progressive era. Margaret Mitchell's
mother might bring her young daughter to rural women's club meet-
ings for the purpose of lecturing on woman's suffrage, and she might
insist that Margaret receive a college education, but this same mother
would be remembered by her son as a woman who "had manners
in a city that was only beginning to know that there was such a thing.
She dressed quietly and was soft-spoken."[19] The mother who gave
"impassioned speeches" on the lecture circuit was "soft-spoken"
amid the males of the family. To Margaret, her mother appeared divided between her two roles and distanced through her contributions
to community welfare. But Maybelle's influence on Margaret was profound.

   Through the guise of fiction Margaret later sought to describe and
understand the conflicting demands made on and by women, particularly in their relations with men. Behind the mask of Scarlett is a
woman who possesses a feminine identity that does not conform with
the identity of other females. Throughout *Gone with the Wind,* Scarlett
ponders, what kind of a woman am I? Why am I unlike other women?

What power do I hold? How can I assure my own survival and that of my children? Scarlett's confusion is not surprising, given the experience of many southern women during and after the Civil War. Many of these women, Anne Firor Scott has observed, faced "life without a man around to make decisions," and therefore became increasingly active in participating in the world outside the home.[20] Yet for Scarlett the problem is not "life without a man," but life with too many men, too many demanding and conflicting roles to play. In the Mitchell family order, the ambiguous and contradictory roles played by Maybelle and demanded also of Margaret were unresolved. Too many men, too many demands, too many roles—these problems constitute Scarlett's refrain. Margaret's life and her fiction were a search for understanding these dilemmas.

Whether comprehending or not, the still very young Margaret was compelled to participate in her parents' demanding way of life. Taking their demands for courage and achievement as her own, she began to ride her brother's horse. Because her brother was increasingly devoting his time to maintaining his successful school record, Bucephalus became largely Margaret's own, and she rode him for hours each day. Wishing to display her skill in managing the giant horse despite her own small stature, Margaret pulled Bucephalus into a sharp turn, as her brother and family watched amazed, but the horse was not as sure-footed as Margaret had thought or she had not been able to exert sufficient pressure. Bucephalus fell, and Margaret slipped off, badly hurt in the fall. Her leg was crushed, and she required surgery, but because of her youth and the excellence of her care, she recovered nearly completely—she was left with a slight limp—from the second violent accident in her life. Once again, Margaret was forced to spend long months in recuperation, under the devoted care of her mother; this time, instead of making up stories or having them read to her, Margaret spent her convalescence reading fiction from her parents' extensive library, thereby preparing herself for the forays into fiction writing she would make in her teens.

The picture that comes to us of young Margaret is of a physically active, self-demanding child who forced herself to physical limits and then was compelled to retreat into literature and the relative safety of the family library to recover from the disastrous results of her danger seeking. She found herself controlled by her environment, forced to attend schools selected by her parents, and always placed as the younger child in the lesser position in the family constellation.

Stephens's younger sister might take his place on his horse and
nearly kill herself in the act, but she could never take his place or
assume his role in the family or in the world outside the family. Beyond
the family, beyond the small local public schools of Atlanta, Margaret
Mitchell faced the large outer world—for women, the world of marriage as a measure of success—and this realm might seem gentle and
controllable on the surface, but it also held struggles and competitions
for the "belle in embryo" housed so expensively in a mansion on Peachtree Street. The success and attention Margaret strove for so insistently
on the back of Bucephalus was to be won in an arena quite different
from her brother's.

In the fall of 1914 Margaret entered Washington Seminary located
a few blocks north of the family home on Peachtree Street and at the
center of elite Atlanta. Not surprisingly, Margaret's best subject at the
Seminary was English composition, and throughout her education
there she was in the college preparatory course of study. Her brother
remembered the years Margaret spent at Washington Seminary as a
preparation for social rather than academic success. To Stephens it
seemed that "there was a social duty on the young men to go to war
(and he did so with his usual success as a young officer with combat
experience in France) and there was a social duty on the young ladies
to see that the soldiers had as nice a time as they could." To this crucial
"social duty," the Mitchell family fitted itself with care in order to
ensure the social success of Margaret among Stephens's fellow officers
at Fort McPherson, near Atlanta. Stephens writes, "Margaret could
entertain these young men. She had a big house, servants, a car that
would hold seven people, and, if you crowded enough, quite a few
more. She was a good dancer, and, just as important, a good conver-
sationalist, and she also had the gift of listening to other people. There
was no girl in Atlanta more popular with the young officers.[21] Whatever charm Margaret possessed as dancer or communicator was out-
weighed in her brother's memory by luxury and security; she could
entertain, first of all, because she "had a big house, servants, and a
car" that appeared more a transport van than a family automobile.
With these significant material holdings, it was no wonder, in Stephens's eye, that his sister was the most popular girl, a true belle,
among the officers.

Amid the gaiety and seeming stability of the big house on Peachtree
Street, disaster broke over the wealth and order of the Mitchell family.
The first disruption during the war had, in fact, nothing to do with

the actual horrors of World War I abroad. While Stephens was training as a cadet officer and his sister was entertaining cadet officers in the spring of 1917, a high continuous dry south wind swept a small fire near the Mitchell's old Jackson Street neighborhood for twenty blocks. The officers in training were summoned to help fight the fire. Eventually, after many hours, a burned-over zone was created, and the fire was controlled. But the financial losses of the Mitchell family were enormous. Thirteen houses, including the home where the family had lived with Grandmother Stephens, were destroyed, and each home had represented substantial rental income as well as the bulk of the Stephens estate. The Mitchell-Stephens security began to founder.

The meaning of that loss was comprehended by Maybelle Stephens Mitchell, first of all, because she would have been an heir to the Stephens estate through her mother, and she had long been active in assisting in the management of family properties together with her husband. Stephens, her son, recorded her reaction to the financial ruin of the Stephens clan: "Mother insisted that I spend whatever of my cadet's pay and officer's pay I had on having a good time, and she wanted Margaret to have a good time" also. Stephens, the firstborn, only son, and favorite of Grandmother Stephens, had been meant to carry on the family name and substance—Maybelle was one of a family of female offspring—and nurture its success both for himself and the other descendants such as Margaret. But now there was little left to maintain. Maybelle told her son, "Don't try to save a dime and lay the dime aside. For all we know, after this is over, the dime or the dollar or the million dollars will be worth nothing. Things have a habit of disappearing during wars, but what you have seen and what you have done are something that will always be with you, and that you can remember, and its remembrance will have a much greater value than denying yourself the sight of it."[22] Stephens Mitchell offered a vivid glimpse into the family's response to financial disaster. What was significant in Maybelle Stephens Mitchell's advice to her children was her reiteration of the "value" of "remembrance," and her insistence that the "seeing" and the "remembering" of the past was the only means of locating and determining "such value."

Loss in Maybelle's version of experience was inevitable for even the most wealthy and successful of Atlantans. What compensated human beings was their capacity to envision and validate the meaning of loss and their willingness to share and relate that meaning to their descendants who would themselves be struck by disaster in their own time. The drama of experience Maybelle describes and her son reenacts in his own remembrances was reformulated through the guise of fiction in *Gone with the Wind*: the plot of the novel recorded constant disaster amid the memory of a cherished and safe past as a kind of compulsive repetition. For the young Margaret's observant eyes, there would be an ever-present ambiguity expressed by the Stephens-Mitchell family: a family that compelled "Margaret to have a good time" and yet that expressed how "things have a habit of disappearing." Somehow both highly conflicting states of experience—the "very attractive circumstances" and the fact of being "worth nothing"—applied and repeated themselves and did so inevitably and without clear resolution.

In the fall of 1917, after a summer of officers' parties and family disaster, Margaret returned to complete her secondary education at Washington Seminary and to prepare herself to enter college the following year. Her last year at the Seminary was no more pleasurable to her, her brother records, than the previous ones: "Margaret did not like Washington Seminary. . . . She did not get an invitation to join any of the school sororities." At a women's institution, group mentalities, whether in the form of sororities or more informal yet just as exclusive cliques, determine social success, and at Washington Seminary Margaret was a social failure by that very definition. Given that she was a "girl who had not made a social success at her school," as her brother notes, it was not surprising that she chose to take the Smith College entrance examinations and to ignore southern colleges where Washington Seminary graduates gathered en masse. Stephens Mitchell sought to remind readers of his memoir that Margaret "came from an old family who had sufficient means to provide her with the proper things for a young girl entering on her social life in the city" of Atlanta.[23] But financial resources and family distinction were not "sufficient" for Margaret to assume a successful social role. Like Scarlett, she "had made enemies as well as friends," and she had few defenders— even her own brother registered ambivalence five decades after his sister's failure. In a city where social life was dominated by women of the elite who sought to exert considerable control and social stability amid an economic and political experience of risk and strife, Margaret Mitchell did not fit in.

She also refused to be shut out. She remained an Atlantan despite the fact that her brother believed that "there are people in Atlanta who

have always disliked Margaret Mitchell and will always dislike her.
Margaret never forgot who were her enemies."[24] Stephens Mitchell considered the judgment of his sister's school friends to be "wrong," and
he recognized that there was "much bitterness" and hostility being
expressed toward his young sister. Although Stephens failed to provide
any clues about why "people in Atlanta" might "always dislike" her or
why Margaret herself would "never forget who were her enemies,"
the intensely dramatic quality of mutual enmity Stephens described
suggests that he was engaged in evening the score. As always, the
elder brother sought to protect the security and reputation of the little
sister.

   Stephens also felt compelled to look after his sister's emotional relations with other men. Lieutenant Clifford Henry, a Harvard College
senior in training at one of the local bases near Atlanta, was brought
to the Mitchell family home on Peachtree Street for social gatherings
and immediately fell in love with Margaret. Margaret agreed to a secret
engagement and began to wear a Henry family ring, despite the fact
that her fiancé was scheduled to leave for France, along with her
brother Stephens, in that late summer of 1918. The actual contact
between Clifford Henry and Margaret was extremely brief and, of
course, carefully chaperoned. Again, Stephens Mitchell recorded his
reaction to the engagement and, particularly, to his idea of why
Clifford Henry was so attracted to the Mitchell family life: "He liked
the soft Southern nights of Atlanta, the drives, the dances, our house
with its wide terraces."[25] Stephens neglected to suggest personal qualities of his sister in his catalog of Mitchell badges of success, but it
might well be that Stephens comprehended Clifford Henry's feelings
quite clearly. After all, Stephens was also a young officer, and he was
also transferred with Clifford Henry to France in early September.
Henry may have even actually known Stephens Mitchell better, and
surely would have communicated with him more frequently—they
shared a troop ship and continued to maintain contact—than his sister.
According to Stephens, Clifford Henry fell in love with "soft" warm
Atlanta in the late summer. Margaret and Clifford became quickly and
deeply committed to each other.

   Given Margaret Mitchell's Atlanta status as a "girl who had not
made a social success at her school" despite her family's wealth, generosity, and social standing in the city, it was not surprising that
Mitchell chose to be quickly engaged to a young man immediately
following graduation from that school of all too popular belles of At-

lanta. She could prove that she was, at the very least, popular with one person, Clifford Henry. That Henry was a Northerner, a Harvard graduate, an officer, and the scion of a fine and wealthy family made Margaret's choice of Henry all the more appealing. Deliberately and defiantly, Margaret signalled her contempt for the choices and values of the "socially successful" at Washington Seminary.

Mitchell's fiancé was not even to become a Southerner—after all, he was an officer in training and after the war he intended to return to his own family in New York. That Margaret Mitchell sought to comply with Henry's goals and expectations should immediately be discerned in the action she took after his troop ship left for France. She carried on with her plans to attend Smith College and traveled North in the weeks following his departure. But first she visited New York with her mother and also was entertained by the Henry family there. Her relationship with Clifford Henry's family was based on this single visit, and Mitchell sought to sustain the connection for many years, even long after Henry's death in France. Mitchell wrote to her father at the beginning of the term, "Perhaps I'll like the North—I'm going to try to like the place I must live in for nine months, but it will be rather difficult."[26] The term of her connection with the North and Smith College was defined only temporarily. The college degree she claimed to seek was of four years duration. But even at this point, Mitchell displayed little confidence in the "difficult" place or in her own ability to sustain four years of study there. Yet the North—however difficult—was her own chosen territory, and her northern fiancé represented a further commitment to that alien and "different" place.

Mitchell's parents were not so sanguine about their daughter's choice. Maybelle Mitchell wrote to her husband about meeting the Henry family in New York; she found the Henrys "good people, well travelled, educated, how much or how little money I do not know, but respectable." In her letter Maybelle was explicitly concerned with calming her husband's apparently deep concern over the engagement of his daughter: "The boy is over in Europe perchance for life. Why worry over what can't happen for four or five years and 99 to 100 will not happen at all?"[27] While Maybelle Mitchell was imagining her daughter's fiancé dead in Europe—her prediction is frighteningly accurate and what makes her idea all the more poignant is that her own son was also fighting in Europe—she was also predicting that, dead or alive, Clifford Henry would *not* ultimately be Margaret's choice.

Maybelle reminded her husband of the fickleness of young love, and she tried to ignore the fact of the engagement between Margaret and Clifford Henry altogether, or at least as much as possible given the fact that she was formally entertained by the family in New York at the very time she was writing her letter. Maybelle inquired, "Can you remember how many girls Stephens has been in love with since he was seventeen?" Her point might be well taken by Eugene Mitchell, although he himself had become involved with Maybelle in her teens and had married her at twenty. Also, Stephens had not become engaged to any of the young girls he had claimed to love. Maybelle was clearly disturbed by her daughter's engagement, and even as she sought to reassure her husband, she worked actively to undermine the engagement itself. She insisted that she would "tell the Henrys when I see them that they must not say anything of Margaret to any one, so as to leave both their son and Margaret freedom to change their minds if they so desire." She also claimed to discuss the importance of being able to change one's mind as a "natural manner of seventeen" with Margaret, perhaps as a subtle means of reminding her daughter of her options and of her freedom as a student at Smith College. In an effort to remind her husband that she had Margaret well in command—and to remind herself as well—Maybelle added, "So put *your* mind at rest about this affair, as there can come no harm of it."[28] What was so significant about this exchange between Maybelle and Eugene was their deep concern over Margaret's choice of a partner; sensing disaster ahead, Maybelle sought to offer guidance and control to her daughter and advice and reassurance to her husband. Clearly, Maybelle recognized the impetuosity of her daughter and the stubbornness of her husband. For the moment, she was able to engineer a partial truce between Margaret's need to succeed in at least one social arena and Eugene's requirement that his daughter marry a husband of his choosing, in his own social arena, and on his own southern territory.

As Margaret turned her back on her childhood world and her mother's protection, she entered a demanding new one at Smith College. Her mother, for the last time, helped her daughter. Mrs. Pearson's boarding house at 10 Henshaw Street—many of Smith College students lived in small groups in houses in Northampton—would be Margaret's home for the year she would spend in the North. On 16 October, Clifford Henry died in a French hospital of wounds suffered while leading his men in hand-to-hand combat near the Meuse River in France. Margaret wrote to her father: "It does my heart good to think that we weren't mistaken in Clifford, that he was even better stuff than we thought."[29] Amazed and dazed by her fiancé's death, and especially by his "better" than she had "thought" qualities, Margaret continued with her studies and gathered new beaux. Her mother had been right about Clifford Henry and, as usual, right about her daughter.

Chapter Two
A Young Woman, Alone and Ambivalent

The Yankees aren't friends. . . . They are pretty much like Southerners—except with worse manners, of course, and terrible accents.

I think you like me because I am a varmint. You've known so few dyed-in-the-wool varmints in your sheltered life that my very difference holds a quaint charm for you. (*GW*, 332)

Margaret Mitchell's year among the Yankees at Smith College in Massachusetts marked a radical alteration in the quietly sheltered, yet fundamentally demanding family experience of her childhood. The mediating, protecting, and inspiring presence of her mother was lost that year. And even the satisfaction and security derived from Clifford Henry's proposal of marriage was gone; Clifford was dead and Margaret was free once more to reenter the social competitions of Atlanta. But now Margaret faced the return to Atlanta from the North without her mother's guidance and support and without her mother's demands and determination as well.

Margaret had remained in Massachusetts over the Christmas vacation of 1918, even though her brother was to return to Atlanta from France early in the new year. The influenza epidemic and the need for quarantine were subsiding in January 1919, but Eugene Mitchell, deeply disturbed by the death of his daughter's fiancé and by his own son's perilous experience in France, became seriously ill. Maybelle nursed him at home, but then she herself fell ill. Much weakened by the care of her husband and by worries about her son at war and by her daughter's own wartime loss, Maybelle became ill and died very quickly. On 23 January she wrote to Margaret, "I have been thinking of you all day long. Yesterday you received a letter saying I am sick. I expect your father drew the situation with a strong hand and dark colors and I hope I am not as sick as he thought." Eugene Mitchell's diagnosis of his wife's desperate condition had been all too accurate; although Margaret traveled South as soon as she heard her father's news, by the time she had arrived in Atlanta on 25 January, her mother was dead. Although Maybelle had been too weak to struggle against pneumonia and flu complications, she was able to write in her clear, incisive tone once more to Margaret before her death. Her son recorded his mother's last message to Margaret, a word of warning and guidance: "Your life and energies belong first to yourself, your husband and your children. Anything left over after you have served these, give and give generously, but be sure there is not stinting of love and attention at home. . . . Care for your father when he is old, as I cared for my mother. But never let his or anyone else's life interfere with your real life."[1] In her farewell gesture, as in all her earlier guiding, protecting admonitions, Maybelle invoked her belief in Margaret's potential for a "real life," which belongs "first" to her own self and then to family, and finally, to the world outside. Margaret heeded her mother's words, perhaps all too willingly.

As she climbed out of the Pullman from the North to her waiting brother, Margaret guessed that her mother had already died. Her brother remembered that Margaret said, "I know it. I knew it while I was on the train. Let's go on out and take charge of things now."[2] Together, she and Stephens would hold their father and their family in an alliance of trust and intelligence that would continue for many decades into the uncertain future.

But first Eugene Mitchell insisted on following his wife's wish that Margaret complete her year at Smith, and so he arranged that Stephens, just then released from the Army, would stay with him and that Margaret would "come back" home to help him at the end of the academic year. Her family supported, even encouraged her decision to leave Smith after a single year, perhaps because her brother had questioned the appropriateness of a northern school for Margaret from the very beginning. Margaret wrote to her brother on 17 March 1919, "Steve, sometimes I get so discouraged I feel that there is no use keeping on here. It isn't in studies, for I'm about a 'C' student—but I haven't done a thing up here. I haven't shone in any line—academic, athletic, literary, musical or anything. Of course, I suppose my year has been rather broken up with the Flu and Clifford's and Mother's death but in a college of 2500 there are so many cleverer and more talented girls than I. If I can't be first, I'd rather be nothing."[3] Margaret's quest for success in all things was, of course, completely comprehended by her brother. The fact that few freshmen at Smith were immediate successes seemed not to have occurred to Margaret and no one else sought to explain to her that being a "C" student during a time of intense stress, family illness, and natural homesickness was a considerable achievement in itself. For Margaret and for her brother and father, her discouraging failure to "be first" confirmed her brother's preconceived concerns about northern women's colleges as the appropriate training ground for a young woman. On 18 March, Margaret wrote to her father to explain the argument against remaining at Smith to complete her degree, and in this letter she chose even stronger language to justify her wish to return South: "I now see why Steve had objections to my coming north to college. . . . I love Smith, even though it is barbarous and I wouldn't take anything for my year here. It has showed me how much nicer home is—and that there are nice places besides home."[4] To her father, living in that "much nicer home" than Smith, it was particularly gratifying to learn that the daughter who had so recently insisted on a northern college, after having found social success denied to her in Atlanta, should be so eager for home.

Without the guiding hand of her mother, Margaret Mitchell determined to leave Smith College almost immediately by her own choice. That her choice was made without the objections of her father and with the explicit approval of her brother was clear. To Margaret, the year at Smith was a disaster not to be repeated. Her reasons for insisting on studying in the North had vanished with the deaths of Clifford Henry and her mother, and Mitchell could find no other purpose for academic work in the stimulating environment at Smith than to please those she had so recently lost.

Margaret's goal at Smith was to shine "in any line—academic, athletic, literary, musical or anything." The discovery of 2,500 "cleverer and more talented girls" than she rendered her aspiration bankrupt nearly from the beginning. For Mitchell reached the decision to leave Smith within weeks of her mother's death, although her ostensible reasons were not the loss of her mother or her northern fiancé, but the feeling "that there is no use keeping on here." However rapidly Mitchell determined to withdraw from college, she had at least attended for one year and achieved a satisfactory record; even more than that, she had accomplished a significant social success in the South simply by choosing a northern school. The fact that she stayed only a single year was all that was necessary. Although her return home did accommodate her father's needs and validate her brother's objections, it was ultimately her decision.

Smith College, the largest of the women's colleges and the one with
the least formal regulations during the period of Mitchell's attendance,
offered a rich college life, quite unsurpassed by other women's institutions. In the 1920s, more than half the fathers of students were
upper-middle-class manufacturers, merchants, lawyers, bankers, bro-
kers, or doctors intent on educating their daughters well. The evan-
gelical zeal and practical training for women's mission work and
teaching in the nineteenth-century women's colleges had evaporated
amid social distinctions and secularized learning. By 1920, prominent
families expected their daughters as well as their sons to attend college.
President William Allen Nielson considered that by the 1920s students came to Smith "largely in obedience to a social convention."[5]
Having achieved the social distinction of a Smith education—however
brief—Mitchell was eager to discover new success. "If I can't be first,
I'd rather be nothing" was how she defined the family creed. Mitchell
aimed to be first "in any line" at all, and now she aimed to accomplish
that success in Atlanta.

The return to 1149 Peachtree Street marked Mitchell's reversion to
her father's way of being. No longer tempered by the considerations of
Maybelle, Eugene Mitchell sought to place his daughter within the
social milieu of Atlanta and to assist her in locating a suitable, successful husband. Margaret's education had ended. And her social role
in Atlanta—nearly aborted by conflicts her brother said she had
aroused at Washington Seminary—was to be resumed, or rather, resurrected. Stephens Mitchell records that Margaret agreed to her father's
plan for her to make a formal entrance into Atlanta society and accepted membership in the Debutante Club for the winter season of
1920–1921.

Margaret's willingness to pass through the Atlanta social rite for
young ladies of society was tempered by doubt concerning the achievement it represented; yet she was determined to succeed. As always, she
was ambivalent and now quite alone and without her mother's sensible
guidance and careful control. Her own inner divisions, exaggerated by
her year in the North, which had given her a new perspective from
which to criticize southern modes of operation, and by her old memories of social competitions at Washington Seminary, became further
heightened by her brother's own evaluation of Atlanta society. Stephens
Mitchell had also studied in the North and had recently returned from
Harvard Law School to assume a role in the family law firm, and so his
critical acumen concerning local society became an important measure-

ment for his sister. He remembered informing Margaret that she had grown up in a town where "first you assume that all rich people are good people, and then, with that as an axiom, all the means by which they became rich are blessed and sanctified."[6] It was not surprising that Margaret's social potential in Atlanta was predetermined to fail.

In Stephens Mitchell's calculations the "white people of the metropolitan area" of Atlanta "had serial numbers running from 1 to 200,000, and . . . each person knew his exact rank on the scale, because his number depended on the amount of money he had." Her brother reported that Margaret would return from debutante parties and ask, "Did you ever see so many horse-faced people in your life, and so many dumbbells? You may be right about those serial numbers."[7] Clearly, Margaret's aggressively negative attitude toward her social audience and sister debutantes was not designed to appeal or flatter. There appeared to be no mitigating, controlling force within the Mitchell children's response. The fact that both were the guests of these "serial numbers" or that they might be influenced by social or financial anxieties not so dissimilar from the very people they held so in contempt seemed not to have occurred to the young Mitchells. Certainly, both Stephens and Margaret suffered at this time from the same financial concerns as their father; Stephens was in the employ of his father's firm, and Margaret was not employed at all. Eugene Mitchell had sustained considerable financial losses over Stephens family property, and yet he sought to continue his plan for Margaret's social success and, thereby, form the possibility for a socially prominent marriage to a wealthy Atlantan. Concerns over serial numbers and financial numbers reflected the family's diminished hope for Margaret's achievements in the marriage market as well.

Eugene Mitchell and his son entertained Atlanta society at parties given in honor of their daughter and sister, and they sought to protect her as much as possible from her own critical temper and from her old enemies among the social elite. Whatever the reasons for hostility— jealousy over Margaret's prettiness and popularity among young men, her sharp evaluation of everything around her, her unwillingness to be controlled by others—Margaret Mitchell was publicly alienated from her social milieu. When the Junior League of Atlanta announced its new probationary members, she was not on the list. Because she had become a member of the Debutante Club, it was clear that the Junior League had rejected and not simply overlooked her. What made the loss of Junior League membership so damaging was that a number of

Margaret's own family belonged. Margaret stood alone. Bereft of the social success she had sought with such family effort and expense, she was a kind of Scarlett cut off from those she had desired to impress.

Clearly divided in her own mind about the worth of those around her who determined social position in Atlanta, Margaret had alienated the very individuals she wished to control. Without a mother to negotiate for her within the older generation of social arbiters and without the willingness to amuse and flatter, Margaret and her family blamed her loss of social favor on the fact that she performed an "Apache dance at a charity benefit and objected to the authority of senior committee women in allocating the proceeds young debutantes raised for good causes." The result was that "without question, at this time Margaret fell from favor with many of the city's ruling dowagers."[8] Whatever the ostensible reasons for Margaret's loss of caste, the effect was the same: her ambivalence toward social Atlanta, honed at Washington Seminary and clarified by her year at Smith College, became more acute and more clear to herself and to others.

Despite the lack of approval within Atlanta society, or perhaps because of it, Mitchell found no concomitant loss of popularity among the young marriageable men of the city. In this choice, too, the young girl was alone and ambivalent. Her earlier decision to marry Clifford Henry had ended all too rapidly in France and had left her with an illusion of sudden romance that few living men might replicate. Henry remained a figure in the mind, a brief, exciting, almost delicate being of the imagination. The young men who called on Margaret Mitchell at the Peachtree Street mansion only emphasized the charm of Clifford Henry's connection to the past time when Margaret had not experienced loss and failure. For they were real, and they made real demands, demands she was not quite ready to meet unless she could define them on her own terms.

The memory of Clifford Henry's sudden wartime death continued to hold power over Mitchell in the months of her debut and her failure within Atlanta society. Her brother, who was to record only brief commentary on his sister's first marriage, devoted a number of pages of the biography he wrote with the aid of Finis Farr to his sister's monthlong engagement to Henry. The Mitchells remained in contact with the Henry family for many years after Clifford Henry's death, and Stephens recorded that "every year for the rest of Mrs. Henry's life, Margaret sent flowers on the anniversary of Clifford Henry's death on 16 October."[9] For Margaret Mitchell the sudden loss of Henry would require such reconnections to the past not only as she sought to resolve the question of a marriage partner in the early 1920s but for many years to come, through Mrs. Ira Henry and through the writing of *Gone with the Wind* as well.

For Scarlett O'Hara, a sudden wartime loss by death and extremely brief courtship and marriage to Charles Hamilton—the initials of his name were the same as Clifford Henry's—form an unresolved sexual dilemma that she must untangle through two successive marriages. For Mitchell herself, the meaning of Clifford Henry's life and death was clarified by his literary representation, although the focus of the Charles Hamilton episode on *Gone with the Wind* is never on Hamilton himself but on his significance as a victim of Scarlett's manipulation. Hamilton, like Henry, existed in Mitchell's mind, most of all. Both men served a useful purpose: Hamilton saves Scarlett's pride and so did Henry when Mitchell was ostracized by Washington Seminary. While Mitchell never married Henry, Scarlett does marry Hamilton and then claims to feel it is "all, all like a dream." But it also "had the quality of a nightmare" for "within two months"—significantly, the time of Mitchell's own engagement to Henry—"she was a widow." The dream-nightmare of Scarlett's sudden relationship to Charles Hamilton is founded not on feelings for him but out of her horror, "mortification and hurt pride." Knowing that "she couldn't run away! She would have to see it through, bear all the malice of the girls and her own humiliation and heartbreak. To run away would only give them more ammunition." Scarlett's response is to the malice of girls, not to the fact that Ashley has rejected her but rather to the reaction of her own sexual competitors. Amid her frustration, Mitchell writes, "Ashley as Ashley was forgotten." What Scarlett is obsessed by is how "she'd make them sorry. She'd show them. She didn't quite see how she'd show them but she'd do it all the same. She'd hurt them worse than they hurt her." The innocent, easily manipulated, absolutely enchanted Charles Hamilton becomes the means by which Scarlett also understands her true feelings: "Deep in her, under layers of hurt pride and cold practicality, something stirred hurtingly. An adult emotion was being born, stronger than her vanity or her willful selfishness" (*GW*, 122–30) What is crucial about the Charles Hamilton affair for Scarlett is the development within the young girl of mature feelings, not for Charles Hamilton, but for Ashley Wilkes. While "vanity" and "willful selfishness" may form the basis for Scarlett's connection to Hamilton, Mitchell explicitly defined her as capable of growth and maturation. She might claim to hold power over love, but love might also use her and beset her and change her. Mitchell saw in Scarlett's character the range of her groping spirit and reveals in this deliberately hurtful young woman the natural immaturity and uncontrolled action of a young beauty discovering herself. Mitchell was describing Scarlett's nature, but also the heroine she imagined her young self to have been. Most of all and even here in this early state in Scarlett's extremely active career of love, she is portrayed as absolutely unafraid. She has the courage to hurt others, whatever the consequences, and also to be hurt.

This is the significance of Charles Hamilton; he, like Clifford Henry, serves his heroine well. For Mitchell, reduced to being unattached and a social failure, the creation of a fictional world where critical old society matrons and competitive, ugly belles are vanquished, became an act of achievement and aggression. In *Gone with the Wind,* Scarlett's feelings are taken seriously, are observed minutely, and count for something. By transforming Clifford Henry into Charles Hamilton or by seeking to analyze the emotional response of a young girl to social disaster, Mitchell controlled the circumstances of experience in a manner she was unable to maintain in actuality. In fiction, the artist may suppress hostilities and reduce fears within by electing the observer's position rather than the victim's.

In response to the challenge of her life in Atlanta after her return from Smith, Mitchell sought to act, as always, in her own highly personal way and to conquer all. Stephens Mitchell wrote of this period in her life as "beleaguered"; he "worried about his sister, occasionally showing it to such an extent that she reproved him for being overprotective." Without a mother and with a father both recently widowed and deeply committed to his work, Stephens feared for Margaret because he believed that "life had beleaguered his sister with problems she was too young to solve." She stood alone in Atlanta, at least among the women. In her brother's view, she "needed a mother to launch a counter-attack on the older women (and their daughters) who had snubbed her," but perhaps if she had had her mother no counterattack would have been necessary and if she had remained at Smith College, such social maneuvers could have been avoided altogether. But the realities around her dictated otherwise; possibly, the financial circumstances of the Mitchell family might also have precluded further years at Smith, for Stephens Mitchell believed that "Margaret was under intolerable strain trying to run a large house without enough money as well."[10]

The "intolerable strain" his sister was enduring was not so easily alleviated, even by the "over-protectiveness" of a concerned brother. What was Margaret to do? She had no professional training; she had no assigned social role in Atlanta's society regime; she had no fiancé or husband; she had no education to pursue; she had no money to spend; she had no friends to defend her. Margaret Mitchell was alone, possibly even beleaguered, but she was not beaten. Young beaux crowded her agenda with invitations; with men, Margaret could achieve some measure of social and personal success, and with marriage to an eligible man, she could face the intolerable strains at home with new detachment.

Yet the marriage market lay in the great social world of Atlanta. It was demanding and competitive, and to face it would require the old struggles of the past. Such social connections, even of the most intimate order, required that Mitchell contend again with risk and uncertainty. Always accident-prone and risk-taking, she moved rapidly to assert herself and her attractions among the men available to her. Although the Atlanta elite appeared to avoid making commitments to Margaret Mitchell, there were other possibilities. But these other potential suitors defied the control Mitchell required. And in that very defiance, they became all the more attractive to her.

Stephens Mitchell was to remember his sister's many beaux and to record his own detached judgment about his sister's difficult choices. Part of the troublesome, and at times, even "intolerable strain" Margaret faced at the time of this complicated courtship competition was expressed, in Stephens's terms, by Eugene Mitchell's "worried manner as well as in reductions of household funds."[11] While Stephens continued to live at the family home and work at the family law office, his sister sought to extricate herself and, in so doing, compounded her father's "worried manner" by deliberately involving herself with a man both her brother and her father detested, Red Upshaw.

Why would Margaret Mitchell become attracted to Red Upshaw? He was a young man, actually several months younger than she, who already possessed a considerable reputation for rebellion. His name Red K. Upshaw was to become a poetic analogue for Rhett K. Butler; he was a scoundrel, a bootlegger. He had been dismissed from the Naval Academy, and he had been renounced, after that dismissal, by his family. He had a capacity, similar to Rhett's, for extraordinary charm coupled with violent and cynical passions. No man would torment or appeal to Margaret Mitchell more.

Always fundamentally divided between the desire for respect and the wish to control those around her, Margaret perceived in Upshaw an uncontrollable force who challenged and excited her. By threatening to pursue a relationship with him, Mitchell was able to manipulate her family and, certainly, win their attention. And by exploiting the sexual attraction she held for Upshaw yet withdrawing from him at her own convenience, she was able, at least temporarily, to enhance his attentions to her. What made this game especially appealing for Mitchell—and so similar to the manipulative pursuits of Scarlett, who was called Pansy, a cognate of Peggy, Margaret's nickname, in the original draft of *Gone with the Wind*—was the enraptured audience of another suitor, John Marsh. Marsh was a young man who tended to hover in the background of social situations. Devoted to Peggy Mitchell, he was a friend of Red Upshaw as well. The three—John, Red, and Peggy—formed an intricately interpenetrated relationship. John provided unquestioning discreet worship from a safe distance; Red offered insistent sexual appeal very close at hand; and Margaret received their complicated admiration and attempted to control their responses to her with a satisfying sense of inner fulfillment and reckless arrogance.

Mitchell's eagerness to assume risks—in this case, fundamentally sexual ones—was restrained somewhat by her father and her brother. She continued to live in her father's house, and she continued her search for a husband. Her choice was Red Upshaw. He would no longer play by her rules of courtship, and now the two would attempt marriage, although one measure of Margaret's continuing desire for control was evident in her demand that they both live at 1149 Peachtree Street with her family. Eugene and Stephens Mitchell considered Upshaw to be an unsuitable husband for Margaret. But they did not publicly, or even privately, resist, because they believed that Margaret would only rebel more dangerously if goaded by rejection of Upshaw. Almost as if they recognized that Margaret's marriage was to be impossible, Stephens and Eugene carried on with wedding plans, maintained an approving facade, and tried not to enhance Upshaw's appeal by criticizing him. Apparently, Peggy Mitchell could be extricated from the danger only after she had suffered its pain.

Why would a father and a brother, especially individuals as deeply intelligent and devoted as the Mitchells, allow the marriage? Stephens Mitchell writes that Upshaw was the son of a well-to-do North Carolina insurance executive, and, therefore, he was "socially acceptable," even promising as a suitable mate.[12] Although he had failed to complete his course of study at the University of Georgia, and he possessed no profession or even a legitimate position, neither had Margaret Mitchell completed her education or found some means of employing her time. Possibly, his lack of degree and position—factors extremely important to Eugene and Stephens—made him more attractive to Margaret, because she did not feel such a failure herself in Upshaw's company, and certainly, his abundance of money from bootlegging—here a quality the Mitchell family did *not* possess—endeared him to the financially struggling Peggy Mitchell. Red was an outlaw, but he was a rich outlaw, at a time when everyone else was poor.

Red Upshaw offered everything Rhett Butler promised as a husband—intense sexual energy, substantial financial support at a time when most southern men of the upper class were struggling to maintain their standard of living, and social and personal risk for the women who loved them. For Peggy Mitchell, as for Scarlett O'Hara, these were undeniable attractions. Despite the fact that Mitchell enjoyed the complete adoration of another beau, John Marsh, who was to act as Upshaw's best man at his marriage to Margaret, or perhaps because of the very attention Marsh paid to her, Mitchell refused to accept Marsh's devotion. She possessed a safer route to a secure, socially acceptable, and personally smoother marriage; in fact, she played off Marsh against Upshaw for months before she married Red, just as Scarlett manipulates the conflicting emotions of Ashley Wilkes and Rhett Butler.

With the passage of time and with greater self-knowledge, Mitchell would dramatize the emotional theatrics of her own central role in the triangular relationship. She may never have actually wanted Upshaw as a lifelong companion, but it would only be after her marriage to him that she would come to the moment of awareness. She actually loved John Marsh, and she wished to be his wife. Her pursuit of Red Upshaw was in actuality a pursuit of power, not love, power over a force of sexuality and attraction she did not fully understand but which she also could not ignore.

In *Gone with the Wind* Mitchell designed another triangular drama between Rhett, Scarlett, and Ashley that offers some insight into the pattern of confusion and attraction Mitchell herself experienced. Rhett Butler has sought to understand Scarlett's divided response and his own failure to possess her: "I do not want your mind and your heart, and I'll never have them," Rhett insists after years of patient and, at times, impatient demands. Rhett considers Scarlett a "child crying for the moon. What would a child do with the moon if it got it? . . . I'm sorry for you—sorry to see you throwing away happiness with both hands and reaching out for something that would never make you happy. I'm sorry because you are such a fool you don't know there can't ever be happiness except when like mates like" (*GW*, 938–39). Here Rhett acts out his consummate need to make judgments and control circumstance, and through his detached perspective, Mitchell conveyed her own view of Scarlett's childishly inadequate and insensitive actions. The logic of Rhett's perception of Scarlett as a "child crying for the moon" is interconnected with his own sense of failure, but it is also expressive of Mitchell's contention that women without mothers, like herself and like the young O'Hara girls, Scarlett, Suellen, and Careen, were almost certain to be undirected and unchanneled in their energies and unprotected from and undermined by their own wills.

No one among Mitchell's family or friends made any effort to prevent her from marrying Upshaw. Yet many of those individuals were struck by the inappropriateness of the match, for Red and Peggy were perceived by even their contemporaries as being fundamentally at odds. Whatever Upshaw's motives for marrying Mitchell—financial, sexual, or the scoring of a social success in Atlanta—Mitchell's own choice of Upshaw indicated to those around her a crisis of identity and a failure to see herself clearly. In his memoirs, Stephens Mitchell recalled the comment from a young woman who had observed the "drama," as it was referred to in Atlanta society, and felt compelled to explain it to him: "I saw the announcement of Margaret's engagement. It's a great mistake. She's in love with John Marsh and doesn't know it." Stephens Mitchell recorded his own strategy for dealing with his sister's decision to marry Upshaw: he "decided the one way to make certain that Margaret married the young man would be to object to him. Stephens knew his sister. He said nothing, and hoped for the best."[13] While this form of passive manipulation may have proved conveniently safe for Stephens Mitchell, it became a disaster for Margaret. Although her father objected to the marriage, he did not fail to pay for the wedding. Caught within her own dilemma, Margaret Mitchell found herself walking beside her father down the stairway of 1149 Peachtree Street with all of social Atlanta in attendance.

The bride had chosen Red, and she had received the public, if not the private, support of family and friends in Atlanta. But that was not to be enough to ensure a successful marriage. Like Scarlett O'Hara's disastrous marriage to Rhett Butler, Margaret Mitchell's marriage to Red Upshaw would be destroyed by the husband's violence and the wife's emotional response to another man. Unable in her own mind to leave home and family responsibility, Margaret Mitchell insisted that she and Red move back to 1149 Peachtree Street following their brief honeymoon at the Grove Park Inn in Asheville, North Carolina, and their visit to the bridegroom's parents in Raleigh. Although the Upshaw family was eager to meet Margaret, they had long been estranged from their own son, and they had not attended the wedding in Atlanta. The strain of early weeks of marriage, the stress of the family visit to Raleigh, and the fact that the young couple were living under the critical eyes of Eugene and Stephens Mitchell led, almost inevitably, to quarrels and conflicts between Red and Peggy. Stephens Mitchell recorded his belief that "Upshaw's performance as a breadwinner was sketchy, his temper grew uncertain, and within a few months he left the Peachtree Street house and Atlanta. He never came back."[14]

The marriage, so recently begun, quickly disintegrated. Upshaw was frequently drunk, and Margaret wrote to John Marsh, who had accepted a new position in the Washington office of Associated Press immediately after the wedding in an effort to detach himself from the triangular relationship. She asked Marsh to intervene with Upshaw on her behalf; when Marsh returned to Atlanta, he actually discussed the planned divorce, not a reconciliation. Marsh continued to act as a devoted admirer to Peggy Mitchell Upshaw, so much so that he left his stable position with Associated Press and took a new job with Georgia Power and Light back in Atlanta because there was no place for him in the old Associated Press office in Atlanta. The essential emotional commitment between John and Peggy remained unchanged by her marriage to Upshaw; indeed, her sense of dependence and her desire for devotion had been enhanced. Feeling out of place, confused by her own feelings, and without any significant role—whether as wife or daughter or student or debutante—Margaret lived on her survivor's instinct and on John Marsh's unqualified attachment.

Her brother considered her situation in December 1922, just three months following her extravagant wedding, to be "bleak. Behind her lay a college career abandoned, a social failure, and a marriage to be regretted."[15] Her financial circumstances, particularly now that her husband offered no means of support and her father and brother had spent fruitlessly on an expensive wedding, were also poor. Caught in a strikingly ambiguous position—not married and yet married, no longer precisely a daughter of the house and yet living at home, no longer a student and yet without a degree, no longer a debutante and yet without a social position—Mitchell's career as a writer began as a means of coping with chaos within and chaos without.

The conflicted, ambivalent response to loss that Scarlett O'Hara offers in *Gone with the Wind* and Scarlett's need to rationalize her survival instincts in domestic and family terms were formulated out of Margaret Mitchell's own contradictory and confusing experience. As sheltered daughter, she later found the nurturing home to be inadequate. As married woman, Mitchell discovered her husband to be a violent drunkard. Scarlett described the "blank wall" of her own vulnerability by defining the depths of loss: "There was no security or haven to which she could turn now. No turning or twisting would avoid this dead end to which she had come. There was no one on whose shoulders she could rest her burdens" (*GW*, 418). Neither Scarlett's ego nor her intellect had been cultivated for a public career, but her sense of selfhood, or survivorship, was overwhelming. Scarlett was renewed to life and success not by the help of others, but by her own imagination and her own "family tales." Although hardly a literary woman—Scarlett is scarcely literate at all—she does possess what her creator possessed in abundance, an extraordinary imagination. For Scarlett, "the oft-told family tales to which she had listened since babyhood, listened half-bored, impatient and but partially comprehending were crystal clear. . . . All had suffered crushing misfortunes and had not been crushed. They had not been broken by the crash of empires, the machetes of revolting slaves, war, rebellion, proscription, confiscation. Malign fate had broken their necks, perhaps, but never their hearts. They had not whined, they had fought" (*GW*, 420–21). The fighting spirit of Scarlett O'Hara, like the total force of will of her creator, was not to be underestimated. And Mitchell, like Scarlett, would be unafraid to use others and to work hard for herself.

In the midst of failure, Mitchell sought success, and in this case, the success was to be won in the practice of art, not seduction. But as always with Mitchell, seductive powers played a role. It was her spurned beau, John Marsh, who encouraged her to find a way out of her predicament by finding a position as a writer, and it was he who made the contacts she would use to find a job. In December 1922, just three months after her glamorous wedding had been reported by the *Atlanta Journal,* Mitchell went to an interview that had been arranged by Marsh with the editor of the *Atlanta Journal Sunday Magazine,* Angus Perkerson. Perkerson remembered telling Mitchell, "What we are looking for is straightforward writing without self-conscious tricks, and it's surprising how few people can do it. You either can or you can't; I'll try you out, and we'll see if you're one of the people who can." The *Atlanta Journal,* like John Marsh, took Margaret Mitchell seriously as a potential writer. [16] Mitchell found in Marsh, Perkerson, and Perkerson's wife Medora, who also worked on the *Sunday Magazine,* much needed allies, friends, and guides to the working world.

Marsh, especially, was not only willing to assist Margaret in finding a role beyond wife, daughter, or debutante, but was also willing to talk with her about her own writing and that of others as well; Marsh listened to Mitchell's anxieties, edited her typescripts, and bestowed warm, undemanding sympathy. Marsh was the original inspirer of Mitchell's creativity, and he would remain a motivating force throughout her life. Perkerson hired Mitchell as a provisional member of his staff for twenty-five dollars a week, and she chose the byline "Peggy Mitchell," not Upshaw, almost from the beginning of her newspaper career. [17] Her life with Upshaw was to be obliterated by a new interest and an old friend.

The young Margaret Mitchell, so emotionally alone following the loss of her mother and the end of her marriage, found in John Marsh and in the absorbing life of a writer a means of comfort and commitment. Marsh guided her writing career, and he guarded her emotional life. As a descendent of a southern elite culture and as the daughter of a prominent Atlanta family clan of Stephens-Mitchell, which sought to represent the remnants of that elite in an increasingly egalitarian Atlanta, Margaret Mitchell was an heir to a particular social and cultural heritage. [18] It was that inheritance that she chose to comprehend and explicate to the world at large in the years following her newspaper apprenticeship. Yet even as Mitchell had the advantage of social and cultural training and experience far beyond the usual, her aspirations also exceeded the normal ones of wife, mother, and society matron. Her ambivalence toward that role had propelled her into an impossible marriage, but that same ambivalence would instill in her the will to succeed in a career almost entirely dominated by men.

That Mitchell would have a writing career was not merely unplanned and unforeseen by those who knew her; it was disparaged by Mitchell's family and friends—aside from John Marsh—and even by Mitchell herself. Her brother described her newspaper career not as a literary apprenticeship with an important Sunday magazine, but as "the years in which Margaret Mitchell grew up. And no better place than a newspaper office could be found to make the maturing process complete and final." Stephens defined his sister's career development and public achievement as an opportunity for personal maturation. He described her success as the result of "personality" rather than talent or effort: "Perkerson sent Margaret on every kind of assignment he could think of, for her vivid personality came through equally well in interviews, local-color features, and the stunt stories that were as popular in big-city journalism then as they are today." Mitchell, the "girl reporter," was perceived by her family as a "photographer's model," a star of "stunt assignments," and a writer who possessed a particular "gift—a rare one, as Perkerson said—of communicating her interest to readers in a simple, modest, and effective style."[19] Whatever the simplicity of Mitchell's writing style, she had a successful career.

She also had a husband, but Upshaw had disappeared and the marriage between them could not be ended without his cooperation. Mitchell was alone, yet fundamentally entangled by the connection to Upshaw, and she could not form a new marriage without extricating herself from the old one. No longer inwardly divided between Upshaw and Marsh, Mitchell was also no longer ambivalent concerning her way of life. She had found a way to move beyond the traditional woman's sphere, and she had achieved her own well-earned success on the *Atlanta Journal Magazine*. The Stephens-Mitchell clan was a reading family and, perhaps more important, both Eugene and Stephens Mitchell were lawyers concerned with writing in precisely the "simple, modest, effective style" Margaret Mitchell employed so successfully on the *Sunday Magazine*. John Marsh had opened the first door to Margaret Mitchell's own world of letters, but she had been propelled there also by inadvertent and unconscious forces within her family and through their demand that she receive the best available education for a young woman. At that point her preparation formally ended, and yet also at that point the need to put that preparation into practical action became all the more acute. Without her mother to guide and protect her, Mitchell was able to find her own way and discover new guides and protectors—and to see how much she required them—for herself.

By accepting the position at the *Atlanta Journal Sunday Magazine*, Mitchell became the first woman in the family to go out in the world and earn her own way. Her father had joined his brother, Gordon Forrest Mitchell, in a law practice in the 1880s (both Eugene and Gordon had acted out their father's wishes), and later Stephens Mitchell joined the firm of his father.[20] Maybelle Stephens Mitchell, although bringing considerable capital investment to her marriage, never held a job outside her home, and yet she had dreamed of launching her daughter as well as her son into some public success of their own choosing. In one sense then, Margaret Mitchell was not alone as she took this first step toward earning her own way. She had returned to the route her mother had chosen; she had found a way to make her own unambivalent, and, ultimately, almost unlimited, success.

Chapter Three

There Was No Going Back; She Was Going Forward

There would be bitter-eyed women who looked backward, to dead times, to dead men, evoking memories that hurt and were futile, bearing poverty with bitter pride because they had those memories. But Scarlett was never to look back. (*GW,* 428)

Margaret Mitchell made her public debut as a writer with an article on skirt lengths in Paris in 1922 based on an interview with Mary H. Gunsaulas, a prominent Atlanta social figure who had recently returned from Europe. As Mitchell and Mrs. Gunsaulas measured skirts, the young reporter remembered that Mrs. Gunsaulas mentioned that she had been in Rome the day the Black Shirts of Mussolini assumed power in Italy. For Mitchell, a woman of natural curiosity and intense desire to succeed, this eyewitness account of Italian politics "sounded interesting and I listened and asked questions." Mitchell's editor, Angus Perkerson, published both stories—skirts and Black Shirts—and Mitchell had clearly found her own means of reportorial success.

This, the earliest of Mitchell's publications, revealed her capacity to fulfill expectations of the newsworthy—she learned that Paris skirts measured precisely twelve inches from the floor—and the power to risk the unexpected yet compelling opportunity to go beyond the conventional—she recorded the Gunsaulas perspective on Italian politics with care and precision.[1] Mitchell wrote both the Paris fashion and Black Shirt stories as one piece. Although Perkerson broke it in half in order to enhance the effectiveness of its two discreet parts, the original version was also effective, interesting, and vividly alive to the reader's desire to discover the expected and the reader's pleasure in encountering some fresh, lively insight as well. These two aspects of Mitchell's conscious method of narration—convention fulfilled and convention undermined—formed the basis for her narrative designs of *Gone with the Wind*. The novel was begun in the months immediately after Mitchell left the *Atlanta Journal* at the beginning of May 1926. A careful analysis of Mitchell's journalism career, however brief, reveals how Mitchell's instinctive grasp of her audience was enhanced by her calculated surprises and her search at all times for precision.

The *Atlanta Journal* was a locally owned independent evening and Sunday newspaper; its competition in the 1920s was the morning *Constitution* and the William Randolph Hearst–owned the *Georgian*. Whereas the Hearst paper sought deliberately to "engage the brains" of its public, as Hearst himself put it in an editorial in his New York *Journal* on 8 November 1896, other competing newspapers began to discover the need for entertainment and the demand for special women's pages, particularly in Sunday editions. As Hearst had declared, the "public is even more fond of entertainment than it is of information."[2] And in the early decades of the twentieth century regular readers of daily and Sunday newspapers changed by becoming less pious in their Sabbath observances; indeed, the Sunday edition became an increasingly popular diversion for many new newspaper readers.[3] Joseph Pultizer believed that his Sunday *New York World* might be used as a "laboratory to test ideas that finally proved to be applicable" in daily editions.[4] Certainly, for Mitchell's *Atlanta Journal* the *Sunday Magazine* was a diverting, illustrated source of features, stunts, and other entertainments, and Mitchell used a variety of her assignments to explore Civil War subjects, Atlanta history, and women's issues that she would later transform into fiction in *Gone with the Wind*.

Sunday illustrated magazines in American newspapers had led American journalism to deal with women's concerns with fashion, social events, and appropriate behavior.[5] They were also then compelled to hire young women writers, such as former debutantes who might possess social connections to prominent families, to write and to appear as photographer's models in these women's features. Margaret Mitchell was clearly an ideal choice to play the attractive socialite with an inquiring Underwood.

Mitchell's function at the *Journal* was to provide the "woman's angle" form of journalism, as her brother later defined it, but she also "was good at pressing the Vox Humana stop when the material was there." Stephens Mitchell would later quote City Editor Harlee Branch as saying, "If I want a sob story, I'll call Peggy Mitchell," and it was true that Branch requested Mitchell write daily assignments for him as well as *Sunday Magazine* features for Perkerson, if the subject matter might match her capacity to discern the "sob story" beneath the facts.[6]

American journalism itself was influenced by the rising status of

American women as consumers of products produced outside the
home, including newspapers that contained advertisements of such
products. And those women also were concerned to enhance their own
social status or, at least, to identify with women who reflected the
rising status of women. The advertisers of the *Atlanta Journal,* particularly the department stores that purchased pages of the *Sunday Magazine,* sought a female audience and encouraged the editorial staff of
the *Journal* to entice women readers with "sob stories," articles on romantic aspects of Georgia history, and features on Atlanta life as spectacle with Peggy Mitchell as the personally identifiable witness.

Mitchell exploited the opportunity to involve herself and her readers
in the daring and sensational journalism of the 1920s, but she made
little mention of the fact that she was a woman succeeding in a tradi-
tionally male profession. Her journalism would focus on the point of
view of woman as bystander to the *tableaux vivantes* of Atlanta and its
highly wrought emotional and social history, and she discovered her
particularly sensitive capacity to witness the Old South around her
early on in her newspaper career. For example, in an early Sunday magazine story for the *Journal,* written some months after assuming the
feature writer post, Mitchell visited Roswell, Georgia, to interview
Mrs. William Baker (née Evelyn King), the lone survivor of the antebellum King family. Mrs. Baker's family was one of the most powerful
plantation-owning clans in Georgia, and as a young girl she had been
a close friend of Mittie Bulloch of Bulloch Hall and a bridesmaid at
Mittie's wedding to Theodore Roosevelt. (Their son would become
President Theodore Roosevelt.) For Margaret Mitchell, Evelyn King
Baker represented the opportunity to reconnect readers of the *Atlanta
Journal* to the experience of pre–Civil War Georgia. Mitchell discerned
the meaning of Roswell to be held not so much by the Hall itself or
even by its previous inhabitants but by the "silence engendered by the
century-old oaks," which remained untainted by the war to remind
twentieth-century men and women of the extraordinary past that now
seemed too silent to Mitchell. She wished to evoke the "atmosphere of
dignity, ease and courtesy that was the soul of the Old South" through
her interview with Evelyn King Baker, and Mitchell did so by asking
Mrs. Baker to remember the wedding of Mittie Bulloch to the New
York abolitionist. It was through the ritual of marriage that the status
and wealth of a Georgia plantation family might be most clearly expressed, and so this wedding was perceived by even Mrs. Baker as a
"very fine" one, which was celebrated for several weeks as various fam-

ilies around Roswell gave parties of congratulation to the new bride and groom. At the age of eighteen in 1853 Mittie Bulloch had married a northern millionaire; she would live permanently in the North, and several years after the marriage she would be joined by her sister and mother.[7] For Mitchell the facts of Mittie Bulloch's marriage and even the point that she and Theodore Roosevelt would become the parents of a future president and the grandparents of Eleanor Roosevelt were not significant to her essay. The meaning of Bulloch Hall was in its evocative quality; it spoke of the "soul of the Old South." For young Mittie Bulloch, that Old South was a place of unhappiness and loss— her father had died, and she and her family had few financial resources aside from the assistance of friends. But for Mitchell the "atmosphere" of Roswell, Georgia, contained in its lovely plantation houses, its giant oaks and magnolias, its old social rituals, was the quintessence of the old plantation life she would seek to revive through her imagination and through her own experience. Although Bulloch Hall and Barrington Hall, the home of the King family in Roswell, resembled nothing of the architecture or surroundings of O'Hara's Tara in all its deliberately plain rawness, they did reveal the plantation ideal Mitchell insisted on remembering and recommitting to her readers' memories in the *Atlanta Journal* and in *Gone with the Wind*.

The preparation Margaret Mitchell found in her three years on the staff of the Sunday magazine at the *Atlanta Journal* was inadvertent, unstructured, and even unconscious, but it was probably the only possible preparation, the only apprenticeship in writing, available to a young American with a talent for seeing and communicating a fictional world even within the limitations of a newspaper report. It was true that Mitchell had received a careful education in the essentials of composition at Washington Seminary and some advanced training in English courses in her freshman year at Smith College, but most of her nurture and training as a writer derived from her experience on the *Journal* and from her faithful copy editor, John Marsh. Angus Perkerson was an able editor, but under the pressure of deadlines, he could not always give Mitchell's copy the care Marsh lavished on Mitchell's writings. Stephens Mitchell remembered that Marsh was an "excellent copy editor" and that "he would read Margaret's articles and take them to her with suggestions for improvements in usage and style penciled in the margins." But more even than the time Marsh devoted to the enhancement of Mitchell's prose style was the critical acumen Marsh brought to her training as professional writer. Stephens believed that

Marsh "was always right—he invariably spotted the loose sentence or redundant word that would occasionally creep into Margaret's copy and escape Perkerson's eye under the pressure of deadlines. . . . John offered praise as well as correction" to Mitchell and encouraged her to think of herself as a writer with a particular gift for capturing characters on paper and making them come alive in the readers' imagination.[8]

Marsh's own training had been in English at the University of Kentucky. He had been a teacher of English, had worked for the Associated Press, and had held a successful copy editor position with Hearst's *Georgian* before he assumed a public relations role with the Georgia Power Company. If the education Margaret Mitchell had received before she met Marsh had been scrupulously designed for social success, the preparation Marsh offered on a daily basis was intentionally provided to give her success with the new commercial opportunities for women in the publishing industry. Marsh was driven to assist her, and he succeeded in making her a professional, financially successful writer.

At the same time that Marsh courted Mitchell with his faithful copy editing, he also insisted that they marry, that Margaret run their household, and that she be materially supported by her husband. As soon as she was free to marry Marsh, Mitchell did so. Her brother wrote that "Margaret wished John's career to be the only public achievement in the Marsh family," and for this reason, she planned to leave the *Atlanta Journal* as soon as a replacement could be found for her after her second marriage on 4 July 1925.[9] The ambiguities within Mitchell's experience of marriage and career were complex, to say the least. On the one hand, she had benefited from the opportunity presented by the growing roles of women as readers of newspapers and as consumers of newspaper-advertised products by assuming a public position and creating a "public achievement" as Peggy Mitchell of the *Sunday Magazine.* Yet on the other hand, measured by the prescriptions of society governing female success as a "happy marriage" and the substantial financial support of a successful husband, Mitchell clearly failed in her first marriage.[10] The only positive result of her marriage to Upshaw had been Mitchell's subsequent and total dependence, at least from her own and from her family's point of view, on John Marsh's love and advice. In Mitchell's grateful acceptance of Marsh's support and in her family's complete reliance on Marsh's capacity to steady their unpredictable Margaret, Marsh became the determining influence on Mitchell's life and career. He was stable; he resembled her father and brother both physically and emotionally in his plain, controlled reserve, and he was totally devoid of turbulence. Above all, he was there. John Marsh was known as a man who was so stable he was almost comatose at times; certainly he felt the need to spend Sunday, his one day off from the Georgia Power Co., in bed and undisturbed so that he could prepare himself for the week to come. He had assisted Margaret in becoming a professional, successful writer, and he now enveloped and governed her life as no one, save her mother, had done. He wanted Margaret at home, in *his* home, and on Independence Day 1925 it was to that home, so unlike the Peachtree Street mansion, that Mitchell moved. She had had enough of independence.

In order to be free to marry Marsh, Mitchell naturally had to divest herself of her first husband. Mitchell was able to fantasize the rapid deaths of Scarlett's first two husbands; Charles Hamilton and Frank Kennedy might die conveniently for their fictional heroine, but Red Upshaw simply disappeared, leaving Margaret and even the two lawyers in the family, Stephens and Eugene Mitchell, with little control over her future. The fantasy of power Margaret Mitchell enjoyed in the presence of John Marsh, who supported and advised as well as loved her, was undermined by her sense of powerlessness at the hands of Upshaw. And Upshaw recognized his power and exploited it. Mitchell's fear of Upshaw's violence was based on an episode when he returned to her father's home six months after he deserted her and demanded to see her. Perhaps thinking that Upshaw might be persuaded to commit himself to a divorce, Mitchell spoke with him and they argued passionately. She allowed him to enter the Peachtree Street house, and she went with him upstairs to her room, where he sought to force her into bed; Mitchell's ambivalence toward Upshaw probably confused them both, but finally she refused his entreaties and screamed for her maid, Bessie. Upshaw left, but first he hurt Mitchell so severely that she spent some time in the hospital recovering from the physical blows and, more dangerous, the blow to her sense of self-control. Upshaw's near rape of his wife would be recapitulated in *Gone with the Wind* as Mitchell sought to relieve her impulses of fear and ambivalence in fictional terms. She also sought other means of controlling her fears of Upshaw and the chaotic passions he aroused. Her brother remembered that Mitchell "kept a loaded pistol near her bed every night of her life after Upshaw's departure until news came, years later, that he had been found dead on the ground below a hotel window," an apparent suicide. A year after the attack, Mitchell was granted an "uncontested divorce" in Atlanta on "the grounds of cruel treatment." She was free of Upshaw, and she began to plan to marry John Marsh and to leave the *Atlanta Journal.*

Mitchell's desire for self-expressive and public forms of success had been both nurtured and destroyed by her experience with Upshaw and Marsh. They had controlled her, and they would control her still. Mitchell's creative life would be devoted to seeking to comprehend one woman's effort, Scarlett O'Hara's, to pursue her own needs and desires while being controlled and thwarted by contradictory impulses within and overwhelming pressures without.

The world beyond the home, where Margaret Mitchell had performed so admirably in her newspaper career at the *Atlanta Journal,* did not then constitute a proper place for a married woman. In the absence of a husband, whether by divorce, death, or war, an individual woman might manage to have a productive career, and it was even true that some women worked alongside their husbands in professional professions (Medora Perkerson assisted her husband Angus Perkerson on the *Sunday Magazine*), but social sanction for such efforts was neither easily gained nor permanent. As soon as a young woman might find a man to support her, her professional life, such as it was, ceased to matter at all. Mitchell herself considered John Marsh to have been the one who had found her the position on the *Journal* in the first place, and she perceived his helping role as crucial to her success. Her public position was secondary, unplanned, uninvited, and unnecessary in the long run. That, at least, was her perception in 1925.

The society pages of the *Journal,* the *Constitution,* and the *Georgian* gave the Mitchell-Marsh wedding as much space as they had the Mitchell-Upshaw wedding, but no mention was made of Mitchell's previous marriage, nor of the fact that the former best man had become the groom. Mitchell had determined that her second husband's career "be the only public achievement" in the Marsh family, and even though she sought to make the transition from newspaper or fiction, she "did not believe she would gain such notice from her writing as to overshadow her husband," according to her brother. Her husband might encourage her to write; he might even assist her in a highly supportive manner, but the possibility of "being overshadowed" by a wife's success apparently did not occur to either Stephens or Marsh. Stephens Mitchell recalled that in the years following her resignation from the *Atlanta Journal* Mitchell began "reading for background and inventing stories because she could not help it," almost as if Mitchell, who always retained her father's name as a byline, became a writer in spite of herself and even in spite of the wishes of those around her.[12]

If writing was an activity so fundamental that "she could not help it" and could not resist its hold on her, why then did Mitchell leave journalism? Marriage, the conventions of "wifeliness," held an important appeal, particularly for a woman already divorced.[13] Mitchell also had other reasons for abandoning a successful newspaper career; she was bored with the routine and the stress of repeated deadlines, and she was concerned to engage her readers' minds in ways that involved their emotions as well. The subject matters that Mitchell sought with such diligence—the Civil War, Atlanta history, and human interest features—for her work on the *Sunday Magazine* would appear in *Gone with the Wind* as Atlanta Civil War history from the woman's point of view. As Shelley Fisher Fishkin has observed in her important study of the relationship between American journalism and American fiction, "Whitman, Twain, Dreiser, Hemingway, and Dos Passos each encountered subject matters in their journalism—slavery, prostitution, racism, economic inequality, the Spanish Civil War, political persecution—that would come up again in their fiction, where they would explore them with greater freedom." But, like Mitchell, "it was as journalists that they acquired the skills, the confidence, and the raw material they need to 'start all over again from scratch' and make it work.[14] Mitchell, too, would be starting over again as she attempted a long fictional work, and she would seek to make it work, although her concern would be about the private, woman's version of the facts and emotions of her subject matter. Her journalistic quest for the "woman's angle" would compel her still.

Mitchell had supported herself as a journalist for three and a half years at the *Atlanta Journal* and during that period she had tailored her writing and subject matter to fit the preferences of her editor and the publishing requirements of a newspaper intent on acquiring more women readers of wealth and social position. Mitchell herself was a woman who resembled the *Journal*'s ideal reader. She might be down on her luck, but not for long.

Mitchell's second husband's efforts to procure a reasonable standard of living and his need to prove himself as the sole breadwinner in the family would insulate Mitchell from the need to continue her career in journalism. After her marriage, Mitchell was free to write as she wished. If her husband approved, that was all that mattered, and John

Marsh did approve of Mitchell's reading and writing and her plans to write more, especially for their own amusement.

Stephens Mitchell remembered the period following his sister's resignation from the *Journal* as a time when Mitchell visited the Atlanta public library for research in nineteenth-century Atlanta newspaper files. She was planning to write a novel, and no one in the family was surprised by her enterprise, for as Stephens said, "she had been doing this, after all, since she could hold a pencil."[15] In the early autumn of 1926, several months after leaving the *Sunday Magazine*, Mitchell sprained the same ankle she had so badly damaged in two previous accidents (in 1911 and 1920). Although she had enjoyed excellent health and freedom from accidents during her tenure at the *Journal*, now suddenly she was immobile once more. John Marsh continued to supply her with books from which to conduct her research, especially in Georgia history, but few books apparently remained in the library that Mitchell had not read, and so, according to family legend, in late 1926 John Marsh remarked, "It looks to me, Peggy, as though you'll have to write a book yourself if you're to have anything to read."[16]

The origins of *Gone with the Wind* were rooted, like all of Mitchell's essentials strengths, in her capacity to survive and triumph over disaster. Here the accident of 1926 occurred during a period when she had lost the attention gained by working at the *Atlanta Journal*; earlier, the accident of 1911 had occurred while she was riding her brother's horse in order to gain some of the attention Stephens had absorbed as he matured into a successful student; and a second riding accident had occurred in 1920 when Mitchell has also suffered losses of attention and love from her mother and Clifford Henry. In each case, Mitchell had fought back to center stage in the Mitchell family constellation. First, the accidents themselves had served to reassure her that she could survive physically, that she could depend on her remaining family for affection and attention, and that she need not be overwhelmed by loss. More important, the response she chose to sudden suffering was to fight back, whether by succeeding in school or by embarking on her debut as a means of gaining society's attention and a large number of beaux, or by writing *Gone with the Wind*. Mitchell insisted on retaining center stage, whatever the cost and whatever the effort, for it was there she could be sure of her survival, and it was there she might even triumph.

Chapter Four
The Creation of
Gone with the Wind

She put them down as they were.[1]

Gone with the Wind was rooted in Margaret Mitchell's careful and detailed knowledge of the Civil War and Reconstruction Atlanta. Mitchell returned to topics she had explored as a journalist and continued her research in the Atlanta public library after she left the *Atlanta Journal.* Yet in *Gone with the Wind* Mitchell's strategy demanded that she go far beyond the journalist's or researcher's role of observing and recording facts, covering a story from the "woman's angle," or seeking to document the past. Instead, Mitchell sought to restructure and reorient the reader's perception of the Civil War world and its aftermath. Mitchell sought to enable the reader to see that world "as it was," to extricate him from preconceived notions and private prejudices.

The evolution of this system of design was derived from Mitchell's "philosophy" of the "case system"—she was after all the daughter and sister of lawyers—from her journalistic experience and that of John Marsh, and from her own carefully critical review of Civil War literature. Mitchell sought to create a novel containing her own vision of southern survival, and she was not much concerned, at least as she wrote it, to pay attention to the world outside her family, her husband, and her Atlanta. As long as she retained the central position in that world, as long as she was able to communicate her own vision of that world in the chaotic typescripts that accumulated so voluminously, Mitchell was fulfilled.

Her brother also began writing about Civil War history in 1926, for he, like his father, was interested in Atlanta history and he was involved in the development of the Atlanta Historical Society. During this time, Stephens Mitchell wrote and published an article on Confederate manufacturing in the *Bulletin* of the Society, which his sister read and edited as she was compiling sources for Rhett Butler's escapades in blockade running and munitions supply. In addition to pro-

viding insight into the economics of Atlanta's remarkable survival and
redevelopment during the Civil War and Reconstruction, Mitchell also
sought to employ her family's training in legal evaluation of character.
Her brother believed that his sister designed characters via the "case
system": "You get no rules and no text, but you study cases which have
been tried and decided, and you find out how they turn out. . . .
When she drew characters, it was not from any preconceived notion of
how they *ought* to behave. She put them down as they were."[2] The
"cases" of Rhett or Scarlett or Ashley existed in Margaret Mitchell's
vision as individuals who functioned on their own terms. They were
designed to bring the history of Atlanta—its economics, its politics,
its sociology, its survival—into clear and poignant focus for the readers
of *Gone with the Wind*.

Mitchell's demythologizing strategy was personal, as her brother remembered it, but it was also intended to be a corrective to the traditional myths of Civil War literature. Edmund Wilson has defined the
terms of the rival northern and southern myths that succored both sides
of the war in his classic text *Patriotic Gore: Studies in the Literature of the
American Civil War*. Wilson discovered in the North's "Armageddon-
like vision" a need to direct against the South a "holy crusade which
was to liberate the slaves and to punish their unrighteous masters"
whatever the cost or consequence to the South. This was a purification
myth; the North was acting out the "Will of God" by destroying the
evil South. The southern myth was a restorative one; for them the
essential purpose and meaning of the war was to rescue "a hallowed
ideal of gallantry, aristocratic freedom, fine manners and luxurious living from the materialism and vulgarity of the mercantile northern society."[3] To restore the glorious past and to ensure its survival,
southerners sought to destroy the vulgar North whatever the cost or
consequence.

For Mitchell, the significance of these myths was not diminished by
Appomattox or by Reconstruction. In her version of southern experience, at least, the restorative myths of the Old South were to remain
deeply embedded within the southern mind and were also to require a
thorough questioning. What, Mitchell, pondered, did they signify for
women of the South? How could the costs and the consequences of a
Civil War have meaning for those who did not understand the ideals
and integrity of those who fought the war? Could the South also em-
brace the vulgar and materialistic northern goals when it had lost its
old luxurious financial advantages? Could any of the old ideas of a

plantation aristocracy be retained in a world caught up in the challenges of mere physical and emotional survival?

Mitchell would focus her attention on the southern myths and southern value systems through the eyes of Scarlett O'Hara. The plantation aristocracy, represented in *Gone with the Wind* by the Wilkes family, forged a powerful intellectual and moral framework, which undermined another value system of economic individualism, industrialism, and urbanism, represented by Scarlett's dynamic pragmatism. For Mitchell, neither system of values was without pitfalls. But the confrontation of the seemingly indivisible yet all too vulnerable plantation creed with the newly powerful industrial and urban utilitarian developments would provide Mitchell with an important means of testing the qualities of the defeated Old South and the potential of the newly industrialized Atlanta through the visionary structure and characters of her novel.[4]

For Mitchell, the needs of the New Atlanta—its industrial development, its urbanized landscape, its social commitment to success in the most material terms, its need to reaffirm itself—required a mythic conception of the Old South. The paradoxes lurking within the old myths and the new challenges would form the basis for Mitchell's theme of survival in the novel. What were the sources of survival Mitchell demanded to know and to explore? How were men and women to reconcile their feelings of loss and embitterment at their many defeats at home and at war? Given a future, given a "tomorrow is another day," what would they do with it in the face of so many miseries? And how would their descendants fare when those who had experienced the collapse of the Old South were no longer available to remind the new generations of the South of the true meaning of the past?

Mitchell began to write *Gone with the Wind* with a design intended to clarify the southern experience of the Confederate defeat, particularly as that experience imposed itself on southern women. Mitchell began to compose the text by writing the penultimate page: "She had never understood either of the men she had loved and so she had lost them both" (*GW,* 1036–37). The experience of a woman without comprehension who was doomed to lose what she needed most formed the origin and the culmination of Mitchell's design. With little beyond intelligence and ambition, Mitchell would transform these into the kind of success most valued by her culture: enraptured attention and the legitimation of the southern point of view. *Gone with the Wind* would purchase both in overwhelming quantities for its author. In the creation of the text she would master the South on her terms and by her rules, and she would define the terms and the rules of southern experience for future generations of readers.

The self-consciousness of Mitchell's efforts was clear from the beginning of the novel's composition. By drafting the conclusion first, Mitchell demonstrated her control over the subject: the "she" was as yet unnamed, like the novel itself, but that "she," with all her misunderstandings and defeats, was to serve as the fundamental focus of Mitchell's assault on the strengths and weakness of southern culture. Mitchell stood at the margin of that cultural experience even though, as a daughter of Old Atlanta families, a member of the upper-middle-class social world, and a successful newspaper writer she also stood at the center of Atlanta's way of life. An astute participant-observer, Mitchell maintained a critical perspective on her beloved Atlanta and its past.

The process of the creation of Mitchell's novel was informed by Mitchell's own experience as a southern woman. She was a woman of ambiguities and ambivalences, of successes and failures, of social standing and social alienation, all of which allowed her to reflect deeply on the meaning of what precisely her female central consciousness "never understood." Through the exceptionally acute visionary power of the novelist, Mitchell enabled her readers to stand outside of and yet to be a part of southern culture. To achieve this divided perspective became a source of subtle self-exploration as well as extraordinary art.

Mitchell considered it one of her responsibilities to fight superficial and prejudiced valuations of the South. The exploration of deviations from the accepted and the obvious drove Mitchell on. The novel begins not with Scarlett's self-revelation found in the last chapter, but with her capacity to delude others: "Scarlett O'Hara was not beautiful, but men seldom realized it." If "her true self was poorly concealed" from the men who surrounded her, from her mother, mammy, and members of her family, and even from herself, Scarlett's inner being and worth are *not* concealed from the reader (*GW,* 3). Mitchell insisted from the very first page of her text that Scarlett's portrait is not the "pretty picture" of a belle, but a portrait of the "decorous deviousness" required of her. However little known that internal self might be, Scarlett does possess a "true self."[5]

The meaning of that self propels Scarlett from defeat to defeat with scarcely time for recovery, and each defeat signals the possibility for revelation. Scarlett's life embodies the southern woman's pursuit of a design outlined for her and for her sister belles by the Old South itself. Her outer being of modesty, demureness, and quietness is challenged by circumstances, and yet her very existence, in spite of disasters, is governed by the rules for success in her society. Scarlett's success is measured by the wealth and social position of her husbands; her failures reflect the penalties exacted of her by her inability to control her passion and her temper. It is the *expression* of feeling that undermines Scarlett's success and brings about her defeat again and again.[6]

For Mitchell, the relationships between men and women in nineteenth-century America keep them in separate spheres of existence until marriage. Even after marriage, differing educations, social expectations, and biological demands ensure that the masculine world remains an alien space of tension and antagonism.[7] Scarlett's explorations of that space, and especially her desire to conquer its challenges, form an essential part of her character. But she expresses her struggle for control over that realm, not as a wish to marry, but as a desire to cease being "unnatural." Her encounters with the men who seek to control her are intense, competitive, and antagonistic. Her goal is clearly and insistently expressed: "Some day I'm going to do and say everything I want to do and say, and if people don't like it I don't care" (*GW,* 79). Scarlett never ceases to seek to express her feelings openly, whatever the consequences or the chaos she creates.

For Scarlett "defeat [is] an impossibility." She possesses the "weapons to vanquish fate," and yet from the beginning of her experience, she is required to learn that "desire and attainment [are] two different matters." All Scarlett actually possesses in her struggle is "a pretty dress and a clear complexion" (*GW,* 73), and there are new challenges when even the dress and complexion cannot be depended upon. But curtains can be formed into pretty dresses and paint can be applied to complexions; weapons once acquired are consistently employed, for they are all she has.

Mitchell designed a portrait of southern female experience as it was. In Scarlett, Mitchell incorporated the demand for stalwartness against adversity, which mattered far more than delicacy in a culture of disaster, where sudden changes in fortune—whether from bad luck or male inadequacy, epidemics, and military catastrophes—seemed inevitable. Women were expected to nurture a capacity to bear burdens, to appear poised and hopeful especially when things went wrong, and to meet defeat with courage and resilience.[8] One of her few weapons, beyond her prettiness, is Scarlett's capacity for passion. If she lacks awareness of the feelings of others, she never fails to be aware of her own emotions, and Mitchell reports Scarlett's feelings as an important source of humor in the novel. Scarlett's first defeat occurs at the point of rejection by Ashley Wilkes, and even at that moment she knows that "only a little true tenderness had been mixed into her love. Mostly it had been compounded out of vanity and complacent confidence in her own charms. Now she had lost, and greater than her sense of loss, was the fear that she had made a public spectacle of herself." Her defeat at the hand of Melanie Hamilton is caused not by Melanie, but by her own expression of feeling: "He would remember how she threw herself at him when he had given her no encouragement at all." And her concern after her loss is not that Ashley would marry Melanie, but that others would perceive how she had expressed her feeling. She begins to question herself, "Was everyone laughing at her?," and she thinks "I'm as bad as Honey Wilkes," whose "forward conduct" toward men had won her contemptuous laughter (GW, 118–19). Scarlett resolves to defeat her adversaries by the very will to control experience that had created the disaster in the first place: "She'd make them sorry. She'd show them. She didn't quite see how she'd show them, but she'd do it all the same. She'd hurt them worse than they hurt her" (GW, 123). The violence of her passion once aroused propels her into and through new disasters to come.

Mitchell devised a heroine of aggression and self-assertiveness. In spite of her mother's tutelage and, at times, even her own horror, Scarlett permits no public challenge to her omnipotence as a belle of the county. She resists domination in whatever form it appears, and she glories in the "something raw and crude" of Atlanta, her adopted city, "that appealed to the rawness and crudeness underlying the fine veneer that Ellen and Mammy had given her" (GW, 152). This "fine veneer" represents the symbolism of flattery Scarlett executes with "studied artistry and consummate skill." By constantly demonstrating in her day-to-day behavior how fragile is the male vanity and how significant is the "feminine conspiracy" to maintain male satisfaction at all cost, Scarlett is also affirming that she permits no challenge to her power. What she gives in flattery, she could take away. The difference Mitchell observed concerning Scarlett's exploitation of the symbols and displays of flattery and that of other southern women's collusion in the same game, such as Melanie Wilkes's, is that Melanie "spoke kind and flattering words from a desire to make people happy, if only temporarily, and Scarlett never did it except to further her own aims" (*GW,* 156–57). Scarlett asserts her will by maintaining her preeminence over men and over other women by transforming every activity into a contest of power; her success with Charles Hamilton following her self-humiliation over Ashley Wilkes reveals to her the power of such challenges. But for Scarlett even this success yields to another, more difficult agenda for power plays.

Mitchell sought to use the life of one woman as a framework for resolving uncertainties about her plays for power over men and ambiguities of her differing and divided sense of self. In this intensely autobiographical novel Mitchell sought to reconcile through the "sudden flashes of self-knowledge" how her heroine experiences the anxiety that lurked within: "Oh, why couldn't she feel like these other women?" Her personal reality was fundamentally at odds with the principles of southern women's disinterestedness: "Oh, why was she different, apart from these loving women? She could never love anything or anyone so selflessly as they did. What a lonely feeling it was—and she had never been lonely either in body or spirit before" (*GW,* 172–73). The discrepancies between Mitchell's inner drives for control and the outer demands for submission, between professed disinterest and suppressed self-interest, created inescapable conflicts. Mitchell sought to reconcile her desire for success and power with the socially conforming structures of her southern, feminine world.[9]

That world is Scarlett's also and in the creation of that southern, feminine universe Mitchell provided an essential vocabulary for southern women's experience. She also sought a vehicle for the expression of her artistic power to transcend that experience. It would be in the possibilities of fiction that Mitchell would find a means whereby she might explore her own divided and ambiguous experience with men such as Clifford Henry, Red Upshaw, and John Marsh as well as with Atlanta society women such as those at Washington Seminary and the Junior League who had rejected her. By inventing a historical formula for the expression of Mitchell's own inner logic, her ethos, her experience, Mitchell also claimed to define the reality of her own time and place. Mitchell immediately responded to the 14 June 1936 review of *Gone with the Wind* that appeared in the *Atlanta Journal* by reaffirming the reviewer's contentions about the historical significance of her work: "How glad I am," she wrote to Harry Stillwell Edwards of the *Journal,* "that you wrote that 'much of the book was contemporaneous with my own life.' You see, those words give me a firm rock to stand upon when ignorant people who do not know the sad history of the South shout against me that I have overdrawn my picture, that such things would never happen, had never happened. But they did happen."[10]

Mitchell's Atlanta was intended to be rationally understood as reflective of local customs, habits of mind, styles of morality, and most of all, rival forces of power engaged in overt or covert conflict. For Mitchell the Civil War was a mere backdrop to the confrontations between individuals in Atlanta. While the reality of that scenery in the distance, of battles and retreats, is skillfully and sensitively detailed, the moments and the milieux of warfare for southern women were her overriding concern.[11] Those moments and milieux are localized through the experience of Scarlett: her battles, her defeats, her open and hidden warfare with men and women in Atlanta embody the larger national or social struggle; the plot of *Gone with the Wind* can also be read as a coded version of the larger American social and political drama.

For Mitchell, this drama records "a sad history" and one that was not "overdrawn"; indeed, she believed that, had she "pictured some of the more dreadful things I uncovered in my research, my book could never have been published."[12] The local textures of Mitchell's Atlanta/ Tara dichotomy embody the larger social struggle between war and peace, failure and success, loss and gain, disorder and resolution, defeat and hope. The "more dreadful things" Mitchell deliberately avoided exploring fully because of problems of censorship are suggested through the eyes of Scarlett as she encounters the wounded in the Atlanta hospital or the defeated neighbors in the plantations surrounding Tara. They were there, but such "dreadful things" were thought and seen, not expressed. Scarlett is a representative for Mitchell's own views. She also rejects modes of conformity that prevent her from expressing herself, even when that free expression might cause her harm. For Scarlett, "there were such a lot of foolish things about life among nice people." She joins Rhett Butler's side of the struggle—the side of success, of self-gain, of hope, of free expression—as a means of private survival. Scarlett's perspective on the choices available is the product of a southern woman's experience in war and reconstruction, and so Mitchell described the play of rival forces within Scarlett's mind: "She was jarred at hearing him attack the very traditions that irked her most. She had lived too long among people who dissembled politely not to feel disturbed at hearing her own thoughts put into words"

(*GW*, 240–42). Within the hidden battles of mind Scarlett is made to consider both the necessity for silence and the imperative of being "far-sighted" and outspoken, if one is to survive "life among nice people." Mitchell was not concerned so much to display the infinite variety of individual character and moral choice, but rather to impose a deterministic and historical idea of type and typicality of her Georgia materials.[13] Scarlett questions the purpose of the war itself, and Rhett offers Mitchell's specialized variant on the ancient reason for human struggle. After the Battle of Gettysburg, Mitchell wrote that Atlanta "expected death. They did not expect defeat." In response to the reality of defeat, Scarlett demands, "Oh, Rhett, why do there have to be wars? It would have been so much better for the Yankees to pay for the darkies—or even for us to give them the darkies free of charge than to have this happen." But Rhett, already conscious of the inevitable and deadly outcome of the struggle Scarlett is just now perceiving tells her, "It isn't the darkies, Scarlett. They're just the excuse. There'll always be wars because men love wars. Women don't, but men do—yea, passing the love of women" (*GW*, 261). Here Scarlett embodies a woman's hatred of the results of war, and Rhett attempts to explicate how this battleground so distant and so destructive might also embody their own private sexual struggle and its long-term outcome.

Mitchell's own South was to be transmuted into Scarlett's experience, "what Atlanta experienced during the war years, the thrills and excitement of the boom town that Atlanta became when the war changed it from an obscure, small town into one of the most important cities in the South; then the increasing hardships as the Confederate Cause waned; then the alarm of Atlanta people as they saw General Sherman's army advancing steadily on the town; finally the terrifying days of the siege, the capture of Atlanta by Sherman, and the burning of the town." In this account of how history became miniaturized so that the novel's structure of action reflected the larger national struggle, Mitchell designed a Scarlett who "goes through all these experiences, and, after the war is over, comes back to Atlanta and does her part in the rebuilding of the city. She lives through the terrible days of Reconstruction and the story carries her, and Atlanta, up to the time when the carpetbaggers had been run out of Georgia and people could begin living their normal lives again."[14] Here in Mitchell's own words, derived from the only public interview she gave following the publication of *Gone with the Wind*, she revealed the priority of description and setting over event and character in the creation of the text. Setting, in the senses of both time and place, was, in Mitchell's own view, the prominent feature of her design.

The world of the American Civil War was to be localized to that of a single small town and the life of an individual who reflected that town with a certain abstractness of character. Scarlett was to be assaulted by the "experience" of Atlanta; she made choices and reflected the temper of her city and her time. Mirroring southern womanhood in transition, Scarlett experienced first the typical euphoria of a young "belle" caught in the excitement of war-time preparations that included her own marriage, the inevitable depression when "thrills" became desperation and attention became alarm, the terror of a civilian's view of battle and siege, and the overwhelming loss. For Mitchell, Scarlett was to be Atlanta: "The story carries her, and Atlanta up to the time when the carpetbaggers had been run out of Georgia and people could begin living their normal lives again." At that point, Scarlett ceases to be symbolically significant.

Mitchell was no historian, although she sought historical veracity in her re-creation of Atlanta at war.[15] The customs, the behaviors, the moralities, and the forces of power within this "obscure, small town" were intended as a complete realm of experience, rather than a purely accurate account of the past. In Mitchell's allegory of the antebellum South, the emphasis was on description of time and place as a means of interpreting experience, not on defining subtleties of character or determining universal meanings. Mitchell was aware of the transformative and interpretive character of her version of the South: "We must tell the truth, we writers of the South, we must give a true interpretation of our section, and so set out Southland right with the world."[16] However "true" her interpretation of this time and milieu, Mitchell intended it to have a didactic purpose; most significantly, she sought to correct northern stereotypes of the South and to replace them with her own "truth."

What was so fundamental to Mitchell was also crucial to Scarlett. It would be Scarlett who nearly snaps out audibly, "To hell with everybody in the South! What about us?" and who refuses to listen to the idealizing, philosophizing Ashley when he contemplates a "Götterdämmerung" of the South. For Scarlett the destruction inevitable to the breaking up of a civilization is appallingly vivid: "Don't stand there and talk nonsense at me when it's us who are going to be winnowed out" (GW, 526–27). Scarlett's horror at Ashley's acceptance of defeat was designed to correct northern images of the South as a region of paradoxical ease caused by too much wealth and too many slaves and of failure caused by too little effort and too much pride. Mitchell derived her corrective theme of *Gone with the Wind* from her mother's own experience of its results during Reconstruction and the decades of defeat that followed. Maybelle Stephens Mitchell was described by Margaret and her son as a woman possessing fundamental convictions concerning the South's response to defeat, so much so that "the past was" strikingly "there for Margaret in hundreds of ways." She was taken, along with her brother, to see "records of the war in brick and mortar. Her mother would take her for a drive into the countryside, and stop on a back road when a ruined chimney could be seen above the scrubby second-growth timber." In this image recorded by her brother, Margaret was seen surrounded by family—she is portrayed as "clutching her brother's hand" while exploring the Atlanta Cyclorama, which dramatized the climax of the Battle for Atlanta on 1 September 1864—and yet vulnerable to the past. She herself was part of the "scrubby second-growth timber" and she would not be able to forget.[17] Like Scarlett, Margaret Mitchell would insist on facing the realities of her mother's experience; however, Mitchell would seek also to dramatize the meaning within individuals who could not respond with Scarlett's realism. Ashley sought to explain his failures by revealing to Scarlett his feelings of inadequacy: "Every day I see more clearly how helpless I am to cope with what has come on us all—Every day my accursed shrinking from realities makes it harder for me to face the new realities" (*GW*, 527). Dispelling this "curse—this not wanting to look on naked realities" (*GW*, 528) was for Mitchell the foundation of her text. Her mother might point to a column of blackened brick of a chimney where once a fine home and plantation had been nurtured and say, "This is one of Sherman's sentinels." And then she would "give Margaret the familiar speech about the difference between the people who had been, so to speak, defeated by defeat and those who refused to 'go down in the world and disappear.' One's obligation to life was to turn in a good performance; that was the hard path, and the only path, by which one attained validity and self-respect."[18] That was to be the path of Mitchell's own performance.

History became a moral imperative. Mitchell's mother transformed her memories of insecurity and anxiety into a didactic message of effort and self-worth, and Mitchell herself would repeat that message. By imposing upon the past the concerns and conventions of her own time,

Maybelle Stephens Mitchell sought to impress on her only daughter that the means of success were in her own hands and that any defeat might be defeated if a good performance could only be turned in. Limitations placed upon women's lives by war and its aftermath are dramatized in *Gone with the Wind* in a manner that allows readers to review the past and perceive *not* a portrait of stereotypical southern defeat and failure, but an imagination of southern resolution and success. Those very limitations become a source of revelation; the precariousness of Scarlett's and Melanie's existence is emphasized to support Mitchell's contention that southern women, at least, had chosen the "hard path" whatever its costs and would succeed in "another day" (*GW*, 1037).

Mitchell's deliberate iconoclasm toward her female characters—one is just too good and the other is just too bad—was designed to explore the critical importance of men's and women's roles in the discovery of the "hard path" to self-respect. For Melanie Wilkes that journey leads to an early death seemingly out of sheer goodness. For Scarlett Butler that journey leads to extraordinary loneliness, seemingly out of her own cruel badness. Yet each woman has won self-respect; indeed, each woman has won the other's respect. They also succeed in protecting what means the most to them: for Melanie, her husband and child, and for Scarlett, herself and her capacity to survive. Theirs is a secret alliance between two women; its meaning transcends all other relationships either woman possesses.[19] Scarlett's connection with Melanie is initially a tenuous one based not so much on the kinship but rather on the fact that Melanie is married to the man Scarlett wants. Melanie's connection with Scarlett is that of dependency and admiration. Each woman exploits the other and, thereby, forms an alliance based on mutual dependency and common need for love and strength. Melanie stands by Scarlett through three husbands and an aborted affair with her own husband, and Scarlett stands by Melanie through nearly certain death. Melanie and Scarlett forge a uniquely sustaining relationship in the course of the novel, and through that alliance Mitchell examines female stereotypes with a peculiar clarity. In that rich network of contacts between the two female characters Mitchell reveals the good side of bad Scarlett and the bad side of good Melanie. In Mitchell's vision of her own work she perceived that Melanie, "the ideal southern woman," is too good to feel the significance or even the simple banality of evil.[20] When Rhett confesses "the truth for the first time in his life" to Melanie, she is forced to focus on a cruelty for which she has no defense except disbelief: "Melanie had never seen evil, never seen cruelty, and now that she looked on them for the first time she found them too inconceivable to believe" (*GW,* 964–66). Melanie is so "full of pity and unbelief" that she cannot offer Rhett any real relief or comfort in his suffering. Scarlett reflects the same measure of incomprehension toward men in her relationships with Ashley and Rhett, although Scarlett's illusions are formed out of her own vanity and selfishness rather than pity and goodness. When Ashley attempts to reason with Scarlett or when Rhett seeks to convey his feelings for her, both men discover they cannot be heard. Too self-centered even to listen to the words of men who care about her, Scarlett shuts herself back into childish self-absorption so that the words of men "fell on unhearing ears, words that were swift and tender and full of pity, like a father speaking to a hurt child" (*GW,* 116–17). Here, too, however, Mitchell suggested a mediating balance to Scarlett's self-destructiveness. Scarlett *is* a hurt child who has never grown up, and she does possess the capacity to "love and hate with a violence" impossible to break and impervious to circumstance. Together, Melanie and Scarlett form their own world, full of pity and belief on Melanie's side and full of love and hate on Scarlett's, but nevertheless capable of sustaining them both with more solid and enduring ties than those offered by Ashley and Rhett.

What Melanie and Scarlett possess is the capacity to survive and to nurture the things of the future, not the past. Scarlett believes that "all southern men, high or low, were sentimental fools and cared less for their hides than for words which had no meaning" (*GW,* 755). In the company of other women Scarlett imagines herself and Melanie, too, warmed and comforted amid her despair over the loss of Bonnie: "It would be a comfort to sit with Maybelle, remembering that Maybelle had buried a baby, dead in the mad flight before Sherman. There would be solace in Fanny's presence, knowing that she and Fanny both had lost husbands in the black days of martial law. It would be grim fun to laugh with Mrs. Elsing, recalling the old lady's face as she flogged her horse through Five Points the day Atlanta fell, her loot from the commissary jouncing from her carriage. It would be pleasant to match stories with Mrs. Merriwether, now secure on the proceeds of her bakery" (*GW,* 1003). These are women with Scarlett's and Melanie's spunk and survival instincts. In their community of affection and ritualistic tea parties Scarlett recognizes "comfort" and "solace" and "fun" and "secure" connection that she does not possess but which she sorely misses. For these women who have been separated from the of-

ficial violence of the war and reconstruction but never spared the consequences "were veterans," and now years later "they talked of war with
so much relish, with pride, with nostalgia. Those had been days that
tried their hearts but they had come through them." Scarlett shares
their experience, but only Melanie understands, as Scarlett herself ac-
knowledges, that Scarlett "was a veteran too, but she had no cronies
with whom she could refight old battles. Oh, to be with her own kind
of people again, those people who had been through the same things
and knew how they hurt—and yet how great a part of you they were!"
(*GW*, 1003–4). For Scarlett, "her own kind of people" are the women
of Melanie's own Atlanta social community, for it had been Melanie
who had introduced Scarlett to them and who sought to sustain these
social connections even when Scarlett was ostracized. Crucially, none
of these "kind of people" are men. In Mitchell's vision of Scarlett's
despair, the only sustenance is discovered in women's endurance and
triumph over loss.

Men, for Scarlett, are always a confusing, despairing enemy of hope.
They speak meaningless words to her; they abandon her when she is in
need; they reject her when she wants them most; and they fail to understand her. When womenkind "had slipped away, she realized that
it was her own fault," for she had always treated women as competitors.
But Scarlett feels that "she had never cared until now—now that Bonnie was dead and she was lonely and afraid and she saw across her
shining dinner table a swarthy sodden stranger disintegrating under
her eyes" (*GW*, 1004). Even the ever glamorous Rhett is a figure of
disgust and self-destruction for Scarlett.

The relationship between Melanie and Scarlett forms a separate female world where things occur as they are "supposed to," not as men's
self-destructive, confusing "real world" demands.[21] And it is within
the survival mechanism devised by Scarlett and Melanie that so much
of the freight of Mitchell's fantasy is conveyed, for these two women
transcend exaggerated horrors to reaffirm the bonds of existence that
have entangled them. Their connection is a fantasy in the first place in
that Melanie assumes the role of utterly supportive maternity that had
been held by Scarlett's own mother. Both Scarlett and Melanie are
motherless and fatherless for much of the action of the narrative, but
it is Melanie who mothers the motherless, even Scarlett's own children
when they can find no succor with Scarlett. It is Scarlett's role in their
fantasy family to act as a paternal figure by reassuring Melanie and
Aunt Pittypat in the house in Atlanta during the war—they claim not

to be afraid with Scarlett in the house—and by providing food and shelter for them all. Scarlett performs her masculine roles with far greater competence and assurance than does Melanie's own husband, Ashley, just as Melanie acts more generously and sensitively toward Scarlett than all of her many husbands and lovers put together. By transcending their real losses, Melanie and Scarlett devise a version of experience that unites them, despite their differences, and that prevents them from "going under" even when everyone else, including their own healthy husbands, "don't deserve to survive because they won't fight—don't know how to fight" (*GW*, 772). They are their own saviors, and in Mitchell's vision, they deserve to win.

Mitchell asserted the significance of the tie between Melanie and Scarlett most clearly of all at the conclusion of the novel. Here the female world that the two have created is broken to pieces by Melanie's death and has to be re-created by Scarlett's will and determination to survive on her own terrain, Tara.[22] Only at the moment of Melanie's death can Scarlett face the total measure of her connection to her: "Behind that door, Melanie was going and, with her, the strength upon which she had relied unknowingly for so many years. Why, oh, why had she not realized before this how much she loved and needed Melanie" (*GW*, 1012). Together, the two of them had withstood all manner of disaster, and together they could have planned for a new version of their future. But, it will be a future without Melanie, yet with her design still as its guiding principle. Scarlett remembers that "Melanie had always been there beside her with a sword in her hand, unobtrusive as her own shadow, loving her, fighting for her with blind passionate loyalty, fighting Yankees, fire, hunger, poverty, public opinion and even her beloved blood kin." Scarlett and Melanie seek the love and protection of men, but the men who love them never possess their "blind passionate loyalty" and "strong shoulders." The two of them, Mitchell insisted, could "stand anything," even death, because of the power and beauty of their common will (*GW*, 1012–15).

The novel's central characters are described as resembling or acting like children despite or actually because of the maturation that the war and its consequences have forced on them. Scarlett, the central consciousness for them all, thinks "desolately" of Ashley, "He's not grown up. He's a child like me, and he's sick with fear at losing her. Melly knew how it would be—Melly knew him far better than I do. That's why she said look after him and Beau, in the same breath. How can

Ashley ever stand this? I can stand it. I can stand anything" (*GW*, 1015). Scarlett is left in control and has Melanie's blessing to ordain the future for them all.

Scarlett's self-awareness comes through the realization of Melanie's insight into Ashley's character: She knew only of "Melanie and how much she loved and needed her and Ashley and the obstinate blindness that had made her refuse to see him as he really was" (*GW*, 1019). Scarlett also comes to know her incapacity to love men as they actually are rather than as merely childish things she wishes to possess, for once she comes to own these men of her imagination they lose "their value, as everything except money" (*GW*, 1016). Scarlett seeks to comprehend her own vanity. She knows that whenever she has had a man "at her mercy," then any "wild infatuation which had possessed her [passes], blowing away as lightly as mist before sunshine and light wind when she [meets] a new man" who might be brought ultimately to beg for her mercy (*GW*, 1017). Conversely, Rhett's final rejection of Scarlett serves to stimulate her desire. Finally, she demands to have him because he would not have her.[23]

By offering the inner history of Scarlett's relations with men, Mitchell designed a woman of self-determined failure and loss and self-created success and gain. Always for Scarlett, the self must be triumphant, and always for Scarlett, the self must be tested. Mitchell depicted Scarlett's battles as unrelieved and unrelievable and at the end of the book she presented Scarlett's dilemma in microcosm: "She had thought, half an hour ago, that she had lost everything in the world, except money, everything that made life desirable, Ellen, Gerald, Bonnie, Mammy, Melanie, and Ashley. She had to lose them all to realize that she loved Rhett—loved him because he was strong and unscrupulous, passionate and earthy, like herself" (*GW*, 1022). Melanie, on her deathbed, has made Scarlett promise to "be kind to" Rhett, because Melanie understands Rhett as he is. Yet Scarlett responds only with bewilderment, for "the words meant nothing" to her, although later she remembers and reminds Rhett that Melanie "thought of everybody except herself—why, her last words were about you" (*GW*, 1011, 1026). Even here, despite all Melanie's thoughtful advice and comfort, Scarlett is incapable of comprehending or responding to any man's feelings: "She had never understood either of the men she had loved and so she had lost them both. Now, she had a fumbling knowledge that, had she ever understood Ashley, she would never have loved him; had she ever understood Rhett, she would never have lost him. She wondered forlornly if she had ever really understood anyone in the world" (*GW*, 1036). Scarlett is portrayed as a woman forced to come to terms with her own incomprehension and her own inability to respond to men, perhaps to "anyone in the world." Even in the midst of Scarlett's reflective experience—more an acknowledgement of truth—Scarlett discovers "some bulwark against the rising tide of pain" in the physical reality of Tara, not in the uncertainty of human beings: "With the spirit of her people who would not know defeat, even when it stared them in the face, she raised her chin. She could get Rhett back. She knew she could. There had never been a man she couldn't get, once she set her mind upon him" (*GW*, 1036–37). Whatever temporary self-reflection Scarlett has experienced, the novel clearly concludes focusing on her characteristic struggle for power rather than her uncharacteristic desire for self-awareness. Her mind is "set" on success once again.

For Scarlett there can be no resolution, no real consciousness, no true failure of confidence. Her belief in her capacity to control others and defeat failure is overwhelming. "The whole book," Mitchell observed, "was written through Scarlett's eyes. What she understood was written down; what she did not understand—and there were many things beyond her comprehension, they were left to the reader's imagination."[24] By creating the inner life of Scarlett through Scarlett's success-hungry eyes, Mitchell redreamed and used for her art the associations and memories of her own and her mother's childhood and maturation. The focus of Scarlett might well be on power over men, but the fundamental connections she forms are derived from her vision of women, especially Melanie and Ellen. These women characters echo each other in words and in behavior. Both reflect Maybelle Stephens Mitchell's own belief, as expressed by her daughter, that "the strength of women's hands isn't worth anything but what they've got in their heads will carry them as far as they need to go."[25] What Ellen and Melanie have "in their heads" is the will to endure and the willingness to risk any danger to protect those in their care. Both Ellen and Melanie die in the service of others—Ellen cares for her pathetic neighbors and Melanie seeks to bear another child—and in their sacrificial deaths they also reflect Maybelle Mitchell's insistence on caring for her desperately sick husband to the point where she herself became ill and died. Like Ellen O'Hara, Maybelle Mitchell refused to have her daughter nurse her and so, even then, protected Margaret from infection and anxiety. Yet no sacrifice would prevent Margaret Mitchell from the lingering wounds within her self. She had lost her mother. Only by redreaming that mother of her childhood could Mitchell discover her way through the extraordinary demands of her own private history.

Mitchell herself recorded the process of her own catharsis in the most significant letter of her *Gone with the Wind* correspondence, the response to Henry Steele Commager's review of the novel in the *New York Herald-Tribune* books section of 5 July 1936: "The genesis of my book . . . lies years back when I was six years old." The words that formed the essence of *Gone with the Wind* "were said to me not by a materialist but by one of the most idealistic people I ever knew but an idealist with a very wide streak of common sense, my mother." Mitchell's novel was to be used to give herself an identity. In the process of self-discovery Mitchell revealed her mother's vision of the reality of being: "She talked about the world those people had lived in, such a secure world, and how it had exploded beneath them. And she told me that my own world was going to explode under me, some day, and God help me if I didn't have some weapon to meet the new world." That weapon for Mitchell was to be "words"—words of her mother's experience and words of her own writing out of that experience. Mitchell concluded the self-examination she presented to Commager with the explanation for her own craft: "I was frightened and impressed enough by her words to learn enough rhetoric to land a job on a newspaper some years later" and also to write the private history that is *Gone with the Wind.*[26]

If Ellen and Melanie exist as a kind of case history of the "wonderful women of the Old South," then what of Scarlett, who lives through the isolation of not being one of them and who mourns that loss as well as the actual loss of their presence?[27] The death of "womanhood idealized" and the endurance of women like Scarlett who possess infinite "tomorrows" to accomplish their selfish ends provides the culmination of Mitchell's text. The Scarletts of the world survive, whatever the cost, but survival is indeed difficult when, like Mitchell's Scarlett, one must face future upheavals armed with only her prettiness and basic survival instinct. Scarlett's is an unheroic humanity. Though Ellen and Melanie might value Scarlett's pragmatic bravery, they do not emulate her other attributes. They, after all, were at least able to hold on to their husbands and were sorely missed after they were gone. Scarlett is not important to anyone.

Gone with the Wind is a private history transformed into a cultural instrument designed to engage the social and historical crises of Mitchell's own era and that of an earlier one. Mitchell insisted on creating her own response to her mother's warning that her "own world was going to explode" under her. The explosion in Mitchell's own experience, like that of Scarlett's, was the loss of her mother, fiancé, and a predetermined future, all in a matter of months. At that volatile, conflicted time, Mitchell sought to identify herself with the darkly self-destructive Red Upshaw, for he at least was there when all that was meaningful seemed gone. Mitchell approvingly paraphrased Henry Steele Commager to the effect that Scarlett "wanted to be her mother's child, but wasn't."[28] Indeed, Mitchell implied that she had wanted to be *her* mother's child, but raised the conflicts between traditional values and the requirements of self will inherent in that relationship in her novel. In *Gone with the Wind* the crises of self and the crises of survival can be mediated, if not resolved.

One of the most arresting criticisms of *Gone with the Wind* is concern with the unresolved conclusion. Inevitably, Mitchell, like her antiheroine, was praised and criticized for being unable to resolve a situation. For Scarlett, there is "after all, tomorrow" to untangle the conflicts within and without her experience. While Mitchell fashioned hints that Rhett would "come back often enough to keep gossip down," the purpose of the conclusion was to not be a conclusion at all.[29] Mitchell considered the "ending logical and inevitable. I could not see any other end in view of the characters of the people in the book." Mitchell's husband and Mitchell herself were "very much in the minority of this belief," she observed, but all the "characters of the people" in the novel have been forced to respond to profound instabilities in social, sexual, economic, and historical categories of experience.[30] No one is safe, and no one is free of conflict. The novel might mediate and even explicate intractable conflicts between and within the "characters of its people," but the divisions, the separations of loss and death, the chaos and insecurity of the aftermath of loss and death can be apprehended only if they are acutely felt. No ending, in Mitchell's vision, was preferable to too neat an ending.

Mitchell reacted to the praise and the criticism her unsolved plot aroused, like her antiheroine, by fighting back with her best "weapon," words. She had sought to heal old wounds by finding new sources of meaning within herself and by acknowledging through the text of the unresolved novel itself that creation and its power to heal and to restore must continue for many tomorrows to come. To have rendered in fictional form this subtlety of human personality was Mitchell's particularly personal achievement. In response to success of a remarkable order, Mitchell sought to do what she had done in her novel: she fashioned a further myth by which she sought to live and to reach out to those around her. If *Gone with the Wind* was the first of these imaginative self and family portraits, the creation of "Margaret Mitchell, author of *Gone with the Wind*" was the second. Mitchell's design of herself as an "artist" was itself paradoxical, for she depreciated at the same time she enhanced her own image. Yet with that image as with the novel in which it was embedded, Mitchell dictated the terms.

Always, Mitchell insisted on carefully ordering the effect of her work and her public persona but sought to create the impression of doing so effortlessly. It is this paradox that is also the essential key to Scarlett's character and personality—she knows herself, and she controls others; yet she does not know herself, and she cannot control others—and it would be the consistent note in Mitchell's own shaping of herself to the world. Mitchell insisted on the terms of that relationship. She chose to have only as much physical contact—and private vulnerability—as she could control, and as much intellectual contact—through correspondence—as she could manage.

If the writing of *Gone with the Wind* provided Mitchell with the means of reassessing her own history, the success of the book offered her a mechanism for further self-analysis. In this case, the self-reflection was effected by her complicated reaction to public acclaim. The success of her novel allowed her to embark on a new journey in new terrain: "Each morning," she wrote to Herschel Brickell of the *New York Post,* "Hell busts loose around eight-thirty and I never get the letters written." Mitchell's characteristic reaction to the "Hell" of *Gone with the Wind*'s extraordinary impact was to write and to complain about not being able to write. "Deluged and inundated," Mitchell sought to understand and control the chaos of her own success by describing her emotional reactions in correspondence with hundreds and ultimately thousands of readers of *Gone with the Wind*.[31] To manipulate and to enhance that success she initiated such tactical maneuvers as maintaining a discreet distance from the public and thereby heightening its desire for more information and forging intimate contacts with such major figures in American publishing as *New York Evening Sun* reviewers Herschel Brickell and Edwin Granberry. By the weapon of words and, above all, the weapon of withholding words, Mitchell could feel she was still fostering her own success.

So fascinating about Mitchell's correspondence is how it allows glimpses of her at once extraordinary and very ordinary life as a house-wife-author in Atlanta and how fundamentally she identified herself with her antiheroine, Scarlett. In her first letter to Brickell, for example, she identified herself in her characteristic manner: "I am Margaret Mitchell, of Atlanta, author of *Gone with the Wind* and I want to thank you so very much for the marvelous review you gave me on June 30, [1936]." She was determined to be modestly self-explanatory, and yet she was inevitably self-congratulatory also. The review was conceived by Mitchell as given to her, not to her work, and Mitchell continued to interpenetrate her own identity, that of her novel, and that of Scarlett without self-awareness in the letter. She observed, "I'm sure Scarlett O'Hara never struggled harder to get out of Atlanta or suffered more during her siege of Atlanta than I have suffered during the siege that has been on since publication day."[32] Despite the "suffering" this other Scarlett experienced, Mitchell was aware of Brickell's influence and of the fact that Macmillan, her publisher, had sought to exploit that influence. Mitchell made determined social contact with Brickell; she invited him to her home; she wrote thank you letters to his wife as well as to him; she asked him for advice; and she created the personality that would be recorded by Brickell himself in a pamphlet Macmillan devised called *Margaret Mitchell and Her Novel Gone with the Wind* in late 1936. That self-designed and self-articulated personality would be formed largely through correspondence with Brickell. Together Brickell and Mitchell discussed the details of sales figures and Pulitzer Prize prospects for *Gone with the Wind* with the zest and zeal of marketing managers in search of an unprecedented success.

That was precisely what *Gone with the Wind* became. Nothing was more difficult for Mitchell than coping with success, for the achievement of the novel, like her mastery of newspaper reporting, seemed only to increase the burden of expectation she imposed on herself. Either success or failure filled her with anxiety. She worried that triumph would be immediately followed by loss, that the triumph itself was undeserved, and that, ultimately, she would be exposed as a failure and an imposter. She simply could not enjoy her own success: "I wasn't cut out to be a celebrity and, as you have probably gathered," she wrote to Brickell, "I don't like it worth a damn." Yet, Mitchell's concern was not centered on the demands of celebrity, but on the question of her own worth. She wrote, "Hershel, sometimes, when I have a minute I ponder soberly upon this book. And I cannot make heads or tails of the whole matter. . . . I sit down and pull the story apart in my mind and try to figure it all out. Despite its length and many details it is basically just a simple yarn of fairly simple people. There's no fine writing, there are no grandiose thoughts, there are no hidden meanings, no symbolism, nothing sensational—nothing, nothing at all."[33] The sense of accomplishing "nothing, nothing at all" and yet experiencing overwhelming success through that "nothing" tortured Mitchell and undermined her health. But she continued to nurture her connections with the New York publishing establishment and, especially, with those, like Brickell, who worked to ensure that the Pulitzer Prize would go to Mitchell.

Brickell's columns on the success of *Gone with the Wind* were extraordinarily influential. He wrote, for example, in the 22 October 1936 *New York Evening Post*: "A week after this novel appeared I made the prophecy that it would sell 400,000 copies by January 1, 1937, and 600,000 by June 30 of the same year, a twelvemonth after its appearance. There is every chance that it will have touched the 600,000 mark by November 1, 1936, with the big rush of the Christmas season still to come." Here Brickell simultaneously self-aggrandized and stimulated Christmas sales of the novel. By confirming his predictions, he forged his own connections with Macmillan and legitimized his critical acumen. "I should not be at all surprised," he gushed, "now to see it sell a million copies in this country alone, since it is rapidly approaching the mathematical point where almost anything can happen."[34] The success of *Gone with the Wind* had gotten beyond the control even of its controllers.

Gone with the Wind can be perceived as an historical telescope. It was published during the Depression and defined by still another American historical period, the Civil War and Reconstruction. Elements of the novel that may not have been seen as primary when it first appeared— its feminist themes or significance as a popular romance—became the focus of study in the 1980s.[35] For Mitchell, the text's resonance among both readers and critics was inexplicable. She attributed the success of her novel of "nothing, nothing at all" to Macmillan's marketing techniques and Brickell's columns. "The column was grand," she wrote to Brickell, "and as I told you before, if I do not win the Pulitzer Prize it certainly won't be your fault. No one has ever done as much for me as you have and when I think how you started your kindness long before you knew me, I am doubly grateful." Here Mitchell reflected on her effort to manipulate Brickell: she was amazed that he had begun to assist her even before she had a chance to use her charm, and when she did use her charm she could depend on him to assist her even further. She even requested that he continue to remember her: "I would appreciate it so much if you could clip and send me some of your stuff ever so often. You know how interested I am."[36] No Scarlett could have enchanted with more charm than Mitchell. If Mitchell could not fathom her success, she could comprehend very well the means by which that success could be enhanced. Her own discretion toward the book-buying public—she refused to make appearances, autograph books, or write anything else for publication after brief pieces for her native Atlanta papers—and her powers of charm with influential members of the literary establishment proved more than sufficient stimuli. The mature, the charming Mrs. Marsh continued to order her life around her husband, his job, and her family. She corresponded with publishers, wrote and discussed her novel with interested readers, and commanded the attention of literary critics. And below the surface of all her success, Mitchell discovered consolation for some of her anxieties in those mobilizing actions. There *were* compensations, but there were also questions. Would there be another confrontation with disaster lurking amid her success? Would she be able to control the terms of future successes? Would she ever understand what that "nothing, nothing at all" might come to mean?

If the act of writing was the only means of consolation and order for Margaret Mitchell, it was also a source of frustration and despair. Even the extraordinary success of a single novel could not assuage the pain wrought by its publication: "One would think," Mitchell wrote seven months after the publication of *Gone with the Wind,* "from reading them [my letters] that I was very unappreciative of my success. The trouble is that I've never been permitted time or opportunity to enjoy my success or even be proud of it or be happy in it."[37] She continued to believe she would never escape or recover from the publication of her novel, and five years later she would insist that "since that time [I] have been trying to outride the deluge which has descended on me."[38] Despite the "deluge" Mitchell could not prevent herself from writing her own furious response in correspondence, but she would never write another novel. Her husband was able to view the "deluge" with ironic detachment, as Mitchell herself recorded: "Some one asked John recently if I intended to write another book, and he replied, 'A wet hen avoids the fire.'"[39] But Mitchell found little humor amid her frustration; in her private "deluge" of success she discovered the death of her quiet, traditional way of life. Having created a heroine with many of her own qualities and experiences, Mitchell continued to identify with Scarlett during her "own private siege of Atlanta" after the publication of *Gone with the Wind*. She believed her "escape" from the trauma of overwhelming success was devised "with far more difficulty, I'm sure," she wrote in 1936, "than my heroine made hers. . . . I only wish I had a 'Tara' to run to."[40] Part of the irony of success for Mitchell was that the novel had been written to avoid the very kinds of frustration its publication engendered. She started the book when her husband brought home a pound or so of copy paper and told her to "write a book" while she was recovering from a serious injury. She said she could not "recall exactly why I picked this subject, probably because it was the subject that I knew best and, not being the modern scene, it was an escape. . . . Of course I knew it would never sell but I didn't intend to sell it. I was just writing to keep from worrying about never walking again."[41] This ambivalence was rooted in her fear that her world, like Scarlett's, "would blow up shortly" in her face and also in her "steadily growing amazement" in the honors, particularly the Pulitzer Prize and the honorary master's degree from her alma mater, Smith College, she had gained.[42]

The contradictions within Mitchell's personality—the desire for public approval that led her to thrust the tattered manuscript of the novel into her publisher Harold Latham's hands and the wish to protest the injustices and misfortunes of a novel that sold too many copies and made too many demands on its author—were not understood by Mitchell's audience, by Macmillan, or by David Selznick, creator of the film version of *Gone with the Wind*. Nor could Mitchell herself fully understand the paradoxes in her own nature.

Mitchell's bewildering horror at her success was matched precisely by her husband's now real concern. They feared for each other, and they may even have considered the success of Mitchell's novel as a source of disruption in their life together. John Marsh wrote to Herschel Brickell in August 1936, "We have been through some pretty tough situations and we have come through them all so far. We have had plenty of experience with adversity and we'll come through."[43] Marsh's response to his wife's success was striking even to Stephens Mitchell, who allowed the text of the letter to be published in part in the biography he wrote with Finis Farr after the deaths of Mitchell and Marsh. Stephens Mitchell and Farr wrote, "The paradox of Margaret's life is in that letter by John Marsh. And it does not seem possible that historians could find another example of a husband referring to a remarkable and very warmly praised achievement by his wife as a case of adversity that they must somehow survive. Even more extraordinary is Margaret's agreement with John's statement of affairs; she and her husband were as one, and he read her the letter to Brickell before mailing it."[44] The "case of adversity that they must somehow survive together" was, for Marsh, precisely the meaning of *Gone with the Wind*. Horrified that her success would create even more anguish for her husband than he expressed openly to her and to others, Mitchell sought to protect him. She wrote to Brickell of a rumor that she had written the novel to support her invalid husband: "I resent this with a bitterness I cannot even express. I would rather have never written a book, never sold it, never made a cent or had what passes for fame in these parts than have one one-hundredth of such a lie published."[45] The fear of loss was implicit in Mitchell's bitterness. Better to have nothing than to have her husband appear publicly incapable of supporting her, and if her second husband was as displeased as her first husband had been, wouldn't he be lost to her also? This adversity might be survived, but in the case of Margaret Mitchell the cause of it would not be repeated.

Exhausted by her efforts to cope with success, Mitchell repeatedly sought to explain to correspondents—and to herself—her own personal myth of that success and its disillusionments. Mitchell retraced her reactions and re-created her childhood, seeing herself visiting "Sherman's Sentinels" and listening to her mother's advice about the "sad history of the South.[46] Somewhat later in her education in the ways of success Mitchell endured a crisis of identity in which she came to discover "that there is a country on the other side of exhaustion. At the risk of sounding dramatic, I'll say that it's a mighty queer and twilit country."[47] As Mitchell gained a clearer sense of what this "country" of fame might contain, she sought to manipulate its resources to her own advantage by corresponding with those who understood it better than she did. Her innocence and yet her growing sense of control led her to appeal to Louella Parsons, the gossip-monger par excellence, for rumor control and to Herschel Brickell for predictions on how to deal with the problems of success she had demanded he help her create. Although Mitchell may not have understood the ironies of her self-explorations, she did learn to cope with her success by repeatedly writing about it: "I cannot help feeling very proud at selling a million copies and I am grateful to people for liking it but I am neither proud

nor grateful for the public interest in my private life or my personality.
I resent it with a bitterness which I am unable to convey on paper."[48]
Yet it is "to paper" that she committed herself, and it was on paper
that she worked out her consolation.

Chapter Five
Gone with the Wind and Southern Literary Modernism

That cold intellect which can write with calm and complete detachment and gusto of its contemporary scene is not among us; I do not believe there lives the Southern writer who can say without lying that writing is any fun to him. Perhaps we do not want it to be.

—William Faulkner[1]

For American Southerners of the 1930s the elements of what is now identified as southern literary modernism would necessarily have been much harder to name and define. The progressive social ideologies, espoused most strongly by social scientists and centered intellectually by Howard Odum of the University of North Carolina at Chapel Hill, and their antitheses, the conservative ideologies, expressed most clearly by Agrarians of many backgrounds and focused philosophically by Donald Davidson of Vanderbilt University, were established over several decades of disruptive change and conflict in the South.[2] The genesis of southern literary experiments in fiction, particularly in the late 1920s and the 1930s, reflected these antithetical ideologies in the concern to reveal intersecting yet conflicting patterns of socioeconomic, political, racial, and sexual debate in southern experience. Novels such as Faulkner's *Absalom, Absalom!* and Mitchell's *Gone with the Wind,* both published in 1936, gave form and order to that debate. Mitchell organized the debate into a conflict of competing gender and sexual demands. Faulkner achieved the much more subtle and less accessible order of *Absalom, Absalom!* by allowing the debate to emerge within a conflict of competing human interpretations of the South. In each text it is debate—experimental, conflicted, unresolved—that suffuses the language and compels the theme.

To represent and to contain the clash between status and class, male and female, black and white, South and North, conservative and progressive, through the vehicle of consummate aesthetic experience is the mark of southern literary masterworks ranging from Faulkner's *Absa-*

lom, Absalom! and *Go Down, Moses* (1941) to Allen Tate's *The Fathers* (1938) and Eudora Welty's *Delta Wedding* (1946). These are literary texts that truly confront the modern world. And they do so by transcending limitations of time and space, by transforming the conventional images of southern experience, and by trusting the demands of aesthetic vision and intellectual debate rather than the formulaic fiction of the South before that time.[3] The southern modernist master writers were paradoxically yet inevitably drawn to design historical fictions. They searched to discover a southern identity in a modern time and place. Their search forced them to be acutely self-conscious and self-explanatory given the South's traditional place in the nation following the Civil War as the poor, defeated, guilt-ridden member of a prosperous, victorious, and successful family. As C. Vann Woodward has written, the Southerner felt he *had* something to explain.[4] In the southern experience of peculiar self-awareness and self-defense can also be discerned a recognition of the ironic proximity of violence and disaster to safety and to meaning and a prevailing sense of the endlessness of battle, whether within or without, and of the requirement that the artist remember and reinterpret that experience whatever the cost or consequence.

It is within the particularly southern experience of defeat that American literary artists confront the possibilities of modernism and transform them into American mental terrains that are modern *and* historical, southern *and* universal, traditional *and* innovative. As Louis Rubin explained, "In the best work of all the modern southern writers [Rubin included Margaret Mitchell in that category] the historical imagination, rather than acting as a hindrance, makes the artistic achievement possible." Fifty years after the publication of *Absalom, Absalom!* and *Gone with the Wind* it is "in works such as these that we can find mirrored the underlying human meaning of the Great Depression of the 1930s."[5] More than that, the significance of the paradoxes that lurk within southern modernism always reflect past in present, present in past, estrangement in contact, contact in estrangement. Thus, Quentin Compson, the protagonist in *Absalom, Absalom!*, "was still too young to deserve yet to be a ghost, but nevertheless having to be one for all that, since he was born and bred in the deep South."[6] And Scarlett O'Hara "in her dreams was still a frightened child, searching for the lost security of that lost world" (*GW,* 1021). While instability and loss inhabit all human experience, Quentin and Scarlett's ghostly, lost presences exhibit an aggravated form of inner upheaval.

The novels that describe their crises of selfhood disclose knowledge of lives "still too young" to be ghosts and at times even possessed of a "security," yet fragile with an emptiness too great to ignore and too vast to run away from. It is a knowledge that could be explained only through a work of art.

Mitchell, like her contemporaries William Faulkner and Allen Tate, who had published Civil War fictions during the same period, had not found much pleasure in the act of novel-making. Tate, like Mitchell, wrote no other novels after *The Fathers,* and Faulkner, who believed that *Absalom, Absalom!* was his best novel, found that it was cited as an exemplar of "bad writing" by the same critics who voted the Pulitzer Prize to Mitchell's *Gone with the Wind.* Faulkner wrote that the writer's vocation was a "quest for failure"; for Mitchell, the writer's vocation became a quest for an escape from success.[7] While Faulkner and Tate understood the paradoxes within the search for an honorable failure— both Faulkner's Quentin Compson and Tate's Lacey Buchen were self-conscious failures—Mitchell possessed little capacity for self-consciousness even in success, and her heroine, Scarlett O'Hara, was designed as a woman who did not know herself.

Mitchell's discovery that "writing" was not "any fun" despite the fame and money came partly from her bitter experience but also from the unconscious revelations of disorientating social change within her region that suffuse *Gone with the Wind.*[8] Mitchell was not alone in her concern for some moral and intellectual framework that would give meaning to the contemporary situation. Her novel's theme—the search for survival by a poor and nearly defeated young woman—was a universal one, of course, but Mitchell's concern was with the history and the myth of the South and, particularly, the tension between the two and the consequences of that tension for women who had no control or capacity to understand either of them. Mitchell's own contemporary situation and life experience was to be linked to her interest in history and tradition in the South. During the 1920s when Mitchell, Allen Tate, Robert Penn Warren, Thomas Wolfe, and Eudora Welty were beginning to write and to examine their regional environment the American South was acknowledging the death of its traditional way of life based on the small farm and the great plantation and recognizing its absorption finally into a new world of industrialism and advanced capitalism. In several economic and political senses the South had been altering its way of life since the Civil War, but by the 1920s, the problem of disorienting social change and the need for investigating the past defined the writers of southern literary modernism, as they came to be known.[9]

William Faulkner would clarify the crucial regional force that propelled his contemporaries in *Absalom, Absalom!* through the imagination of Quentin Compson: "Maybe nothing ever happens once and is finished. Maybe happens never once but like ripples may be on water after the pebble sinks, the ripples moving on, spreading, the pool attached by a narrow umbilical water-cord to the next pool which the first pool feeds, has fed, did feed, let this second pool contain a different temperature of water."[10] For southern modernists the possibility that "nothing even happens once and is finished" would engender the resources of a consciousness regionally defined and ordered, but never limited or confined. There could simply be some other "different temperature" of significance in that shared history. Faulkner described the "heritage" of the southern writer as "a matter of violent partisanship, in which the writer unconsciously writes into every line and phrase his violent despairs and rages and frustrations or his violent prophesies of still more violent hopes."[11] The experience of the southern writer that Faulkner designs may reflect more on Mitchell's unconscious expression of despair, frustration, and hope than on his own infinitely more complex, contradictory, and subtly ironic vision of himself. Faulkner's creation of self and his design of art revealed an awareness of narrative observation, of self-creation, that is filtered through a consciousness of an "other" and of others.

Mitchell, for all her willingness to charm and manipulate, remained a writer without self-consciousness, just as she designed her single and single-minded heroine as a woman unable to understand herself or even those she loved. For Faulkner the range of southern modernism would enable him to test the temperatures of many histories of the South. He would design the voices of those histories to embody hatred, indifference, and awe, and those voices would speak all at the same time and all in the same creative vision.

Mitchell's space in the terrain of southern literary modernism has been largely left unexplored. Her critics have generally ignored the parallels between *Gone with the Wind* and other texts, such as Faulkner's *Absalom, Absalom!,* Tate's *The Fathers,* and Welty's *Delta Wedding,* which share with Mitchell's work a vision of southern history as a source of human consciousness. Even when such thematic interconnections are perceived, the results would not necessarily be enlightening, partly because even fine critics of *Gone with the Wind* seem to have a quite superficial grasp of the text. For example, Louis D. Rubin, Jr., writes in his important essay on the relationship between *Gone with the Wind* and *Absalom, Absalom!*: "I don't think that it ever occurred to Margaret Mitchell that she couldn't recreate the past, so long as she was faithful enough to her documentation. The result is that she gave us a novel with a very modern heroine in lace and crinoline, whom she felt she had to punish for her emancipated attitudes by taking her lover away." In Rubin's essay "Scarlett O'Hara and the Two Quentin Compsons," he focused almost entirely on the text of *Absalom, Absalom!* after making the point that "there are certain startling similarities [to *Gone with the Wind*] in *Absalom, Absalom!*" in theme, in the characterization of Sutpen compared to Scarlett, in historical subject matter, and in melodramatic intensity.[12] Although Rubin's analysis of *Absalom, Absalom!* contained richly suggestive ideas about Faulkner's method of structural narration, Rubin offered little of the conscientious and detailed knowledge of Mitchell herself or of her text that he provided so copiously for Faulkner. For example, there was no reason for and no record of Mitchell attempting to "recreate the past" merely by being faithful to documentation in *Gone with the Wind*. She repeatedly indicated both within the novel and in her few published statements on her work that her concern was to elicit from history a vision of survival that held clear implications for her own generation and, she believed, for every generation. Scarlett was not a "Jazz Age Flapper" disguised in "lace and crinoline" who must pay a price by losing Rhett, but a woman of complexity and ambivalence who suffered deeply and fought valiantly for her children and for Melanie's children. The loss of Rhett was by no means fixed as a punishment but intended as a source of revelation; even that loss was not assured, for Rhett himself promised to "come back often enough to keep gossip down" (*GW*, 1034–35). Mitchell herself refused to create anything but an ambivalent conclusion to her novel despite the entreaties of her publisher to add another page to the novel and clarify the terms of the ending.[13]

The crucial failure of much Mitchell criticism, however, was not that the text of *Gone with the Wind*, aside from a few potent phrases, would be unexamined or that critics would confuse the novel with its film version. What underlay the misreadings and misjudgments of Mitchell's work was the continuing underestimation of Mitchell as a literary artist. Thus, Rubin wrote, "If Margaret Mitchell ever read William Faulkner, I do not know of it; if nothing else she must have encountered his stories in the *Saturday Evening Post*."[14] Yet Mitchell in a letter to Herschel Brickell (later published in a volume of correspondence that itself was a best-seller in 1976) asked for a "review of William Faulkner's latest," *Absalom, Absalom!*, because she would not have time to read the new novel in the "deluge" of the publication of *Gone with the Wind*. Later, she wrote to Faulkner himself to enclose a copy of the reproduction of the dust jacket to Faulkner's *Sanctuary* in its Italian edition that she had received from their common publisher in Italy, Arnoldo Mondadori. In Mitchell's letter to Faulkner, she observed that she had shown the picture "to a friend who is a great admirer of your books."[15] Clear evidence reveals that Mitchell had followed Faulkner's career with care for many years. Mitchell did not isolate herself from the contemporary literary world, and she did perceive herself as a conscious craftsman of the plain style. For Mitchell, as for Faulkner, Tate, and Welty, the historical imagination made the artistic achievement possible because it provided a means of responding to the necessity for and impossibility of change within southern experience.

Clearly, the means of response varied enormously from writer to writer as they drew on the same resources of history for the subject matter of their narratives and in the formulation of the moral and intellectual frameworks of their writings. Invariably, as Richard Gray has observed, "these resources meant different things for each of them," and they "each had different priorities of value, quite separate ideas of what, exactly, the significant in experience was."[16] Concerned with the history and the myth of the South, Faulkner designed a multifaceted vision in *Absalom, Absalom!*, which he later noted was created to reveal that "no one individual can look at truth. It blinds you. You look at it and you see one phase of it. Someone else looks at it and sees a slightly awry phase of it. But taken all together, the truth is in what they saw though nobody saw the truth intact."[17] In the direct narrative sense, *Absalom, Absalom!* was Sutpen's story, just as *Gone with the Wind* was Scarlett's; yet Faulkner concentrated on reflecting the varied and even violent shapes of Sutpen in the minds of Shreve, Quentin, and Miss Rosa. They would be fascinated, but they would also be seen to encounter an unknown and unknowable experience of being. It would be the effect of Sutpen on the imagination of the observer, including the readers of *Absalom, Absalom!*, that Faulkner sought to determine. The aesthetic experience itself would be the compelling mechanism of connection with the past, in which all are "trying to make a rug on the same loom only each one wants to weave his own pattern into the rug; and it can't matter, you know that, or the Ones that set up the loom would have arranged things a little better, and yet it must matter because you keep on trying or having to keep on trying."[18] This novel and the novels of Faulkner's contemporary literary artists became patterns in the complex texture of southern literary modernism.

Mitchell's aesthetic and her guiding idea were different from Faulkner's, but she shared with him an interest in history and tradition that would be initiated through a catalytic image from the past. For Faulkner, the idea of a novel began "with the thought, the image of a character, or with an anecdote, and even in the same breath, almost like lightning, it begins to take a shape that he can see."[19] According to Faulkner, the initiating image of *Absalom, Absalom!* was Sutpen—"the idea of a man who wanted sons and got sons who destroyed him. The other characters I had to get out of the attic to tell the story of Sutpen."[20] Sutpen, the 'boy-symbol" of humiliation and defeat, became a man of elusive and self-destructive power. For Mitchell, a similar artistic feature was to be remembered as the "lightning" of her creative method. Scarlett was to be the girl-symbol of incomprehension and failure in love who became a woman of ambivalent yet undeniable ability to survive.

In both Mitchell's and Faulkner's vision of historical crisis within the South, the literary artists used history to form their own Gothic moments of exaggeration, recognition, truth, and, ultimately, disillusion within their fictions.[21] Also, in both *Gone with the Wind* and *Absalom, Absalom!,* key elements within the exposition of character are revealed in characteristic Gothic fashion through the developing experience of an unknowing young girl who refuses to be used by men. Rosa Coldfield, like Scarlett O'Hara, is forced to live within a world dominated by nearly uninhibited masculine violence, and both women provide a feminine perspective on the "designs" and the destructions men have created for them to endure. Both rejecting and rejected, Rosa and Scarlett haunt the men who sought to love them and are themselves complicit in their desolation and the loneliness left to them in the conclusions of the novels. Mitchell and Faulkner devised equivocal feminine beings who live out their lives as if exorcising demons of the past. Neither woman can ever fully understand the crises she is compelled to experience, and so the work of both female characters becomes the interpretation of men, of attempts to explain them, and of efforts to make sense and take control of them.

What's so fascinating about both Faulkner's and Mitchell's portrayals of women's responses to the effects of masculine violence—the Civil War and the hard times that followed it in the South were only the most clear-cut examples of male-dominated and male-created destruction—is the conflicted attitudes toward female sexuality that appear in *Absalom, Absalom!* and in *Gone with the Wind*.[22] The ironies implicit in the characters of Rosa and Scarlett reinforce those conflicts, and those very conflicts over women's power and women's futility form the essentially unresolved movement in both novels.

The limits of resolution and the continual frustration of human desires to know, to understand, or to complete a motivation are the core of *Absalom, Absalom!*. Mitchell's *Gone with the Wind* contains some of the same devices of suspense and of the withholding of narrative facts, but Mitchell never achieved the totality of effect, the range of vision, and depth of insight Faulkner devised with such seeming ease and grace in *Absalom, Absalom!* The crucial significance of her novel is its "simplicity" and its capacity to speak clearly, even "colloquially" to its readers: "Complete simplicity [was what] I wanted. Simplicity of ideas, of contraction, of words."[23] Thus, Mitchell could be seen to weave her pattern in the "rug" of southern literary modernism in a method diametrically opposed to Faulkner's. Yet if one sought simplicity and the other sought complexity, that would not mean they did not cover the same ground and material, even the same intensely colored and vividly designed embodiments of southern individualism and southern crisis.

The terrain Mitchell and Faulkner shared was inhabited by other quieter, less intense explorers of that landscape. Allen Tate wrote *The Fathers* during the same period *Absalom, Absalom!* and *Gone with the Wind* were written (although *The Fathers* wasn't published until 1938), and in it he, too, sought to dramatize the myth and history of his South. Faulkner's space was what Faulkner called his "postage stamp of native soil."[24] Tate's was of a memory, of "the objects around which secretly the emotions have ordered themselves in memory."[25] Like Mitchell, Tate focused on the disintegration of antebellum society through the eyes of a single observer, Lacey Buchan. The personal history of the Buchans, like that of the O'Haras, is representative of the larger history of the South. For Tate, as for Faulkner and Mitchell, that history is of a civilization they had not truly known. The war they described—no matter how real to them—was one they had not actually fought. A recognition of the underlying tensions, of melancholy and charm, characterized Tate's vision of ambiguity in *The Fathers*.

Lacey Buchan, the single teller of Tate's tale of the South, recalled the years of his childhood and youth as an older man, much in the manner of Scarlett O'Hara's reminiscences at the end of *Gone with the Wind*. And Buchan shared with Scarlett his sense of loss, both highly personal and piteously unhappy. The radical disjunction Buchan felt between the past before the war and the present destroyed by the war was explored as a closely created wound inside the self that could not be healed; it must simply be survived. That wound was part of his own history as well as that of his southern culture.[26]

Tate sought to communicate Buchan's calm, yet tortured memory of loss: "That memory is not what happened in the year 1860 but is rather a few symbols, a voice, a tree, a gun shining on the wall—symbols that will preserve only so much of the old life as they may, in their own mysterious history, consent to bear."[27] Buchan's mystery is held by his father, grandfather, great-grandfather, and other ancestors and is to be passed on down to him by those fathers of the past. Like the many mothers of *Gone with the Wind*—Ellen, Melanie, Mammy, and the old women of Atlanta—these ancestral figures create a world of abstractions, codes, creeds, rules, and formulas for human conduct designed to protect and sustain that life held in memory. For Buchan, it seems that in the past "our lives were eternally balanced upon a pedestal below which lay an abyss that I could not name. Within that invisible tension my father knew the moves of an intricate game that he expected everybody to play. That, I think, was because everything he was and felt was in the game itself."[28] The Buchan family possesses knowledge of the "intricate game" of conduct and they try to give that knowledge to their descendants. What they have to give is "an idea, a cause, an action in which personality could be extinguished"; it is this gift that creates "the Confederate cause."[29] George Posey, the lover of the Buchans' only daughter and their antagonist in all things, "did not recognize the assumptions of the game." Posey could be seen as a kind of substitute being, a man who poses for those who do not know the rules and those who do not understand "the cause"; he, like the novel's readers, may not have had a father so knowledgeable of and adherent to the protocols of the past. He appears as a man consumed by feelings: "With his exacerbated nerves he was constantly receiving impressions out of the chasm that yawns beneath lovers; therefore he may have had a secret brutality for her [Susan Buchan] when they were alone. Excessively refined persons have a communion with the abyss; but is not civilization the agreement, slowly arrived at, to let the abyss alone?"[30]

For Tate, the "abyss" demanded the construction of a game of avoidance. *The Fathers* was itself the construction of a myth of that game, created out of a sense of loss and out of the symbols of memory. The disintegration of the Buchan family is accomplished partly by the arriviste, George Posey, a poseur who does not know truly what he is trying to represent, only what he wants to win, and partly by the Civil War, which divides the old family loyalties and destroys the old family estate. Family and polity share in the dissolution, as the private and the collective aspects of Tate's vision of the South are now recollected in tranquility and in confirmation of values that have been all but lost. Only works of art seem capable of containing and revivifying "the emotions that have ordered themselves in memory." For Tate, whose vision would be restricted almost entirely to a masculine view, the objects and symbols of art provided the only sure source of survival in his South.

While Tate's novel, like Faulkner's *Absalom, Absalom!*, contains a range of parallels with Mitchell's, neither Tate nor Faulkner's Civil War and family war fictions would find wide audiences. Both Tate and Faulkner emphasized the ambiguities within their versions of southern experience, and neither writer sought to explore fully the effect of history on women's experience, particularly with the creation of marriage and family. Faulkner provided an important and revealing portrait of one such victimized woman, Miss Rosa, and Tate examined at least peripherally the failure of Susan Buchan Posey to achieve her own happiness or even her own sanity amid the multiple crises of the men around her. Yet in both *Absalom, Absalom!* and *The Fathers* masculine violence and masculine determination crushes the spirit and hope of women. For Mitchell, the reverse would apply. Nothing, no amount of masculine dominance or masculine force could reduce Scarlett O'Hara's capacity to survive; indeed, such domination challenges her all the more. Nor would the convoluted and complex organizations of Tate's and Faulkner's novels be mirrored in *Gone with the Wind*. The progressive piecing together of events and interpretations so crucial to Tate's and Faulkner's explorations of the myths and memories from their own Souths are entirely absent in Mitchell. Far from seeking to experiment with complexity, Mitchell sought to experiment with simplicity. All three artists sought experimentation for its own sake, but their angles of departure from the conventions of southern literature (conventions followed in texts such as Stark Young's *So Red the Rose*, Caroline Miller's *Lamb in His Bosom*, and Ellen Glasgow's *Barren Ground*, which were extraordinarily popular) provided them with the means of assessing as well as describing southern traditions of history and society.

Mitchell's critical achievement was to create women-centered fiction, and the central woman is "not beautiful"; indeed, she is not even much of a lady. What she is and what she wants to be is her own self: "Her eyes were her own" (*GW*, 3–4). When Allen Tate explored critically the domain of another such strong-willed young woman, he employed the precise words of Mitchell. Lacy Buchan describes his sister Susan, "My sister was not beautiful," and immediately after that statement Lacy reveals how Susan's future life would be blighted by her experience as a southern woman schooled in self-control yet divided by inner demands. Susan requests that her fiancé, George Posey, attend her mother's funeral, but he refuses: "'No, damn it!' Her fingers lingered on his sleeve. She withdrew them, clenched them at her side, and turned so quickly that I heard her hoops swish under the heavy black silk of her skirt. Ladies did not run in those days, but she very nearly ran."[31] Tate indicated subtly and poignantly the dilemma of the "not beautiful" belles who clench their hands and withdraw by escaping within—in Susan's case the only ultimate place to run to is madness—because they do not possess the means to overcome the ambivalence and powerlessness around and inside them. "Ladies did not run in those days," Tate explained as Mitchell explained, and yet both Tate and Mitchell examined the reality that some ladies "very nearly ran" in order to survive or to escape the turbulence and terror imposed on them.

For Tate and for Mitchell, and also for Faulkner, the novel became a way of knowing and evaluating the forms of historical consciousness. Both Tate and Faulkner sought to understand and to communicate the tragic and often violent constraints on women in the South, and the narratives of Miss Rosa and Susan Buchan Posey seem to substantiate that awareness. Mitchell's Scarlett became the quintessence of that experience with all its tragic and self-destructive elements.

Neither Tate nor Faulkner mined veins of humor in the historical visions of *The Fathers* or of *Absalom, Absalom!*, and Mitchell found little comic relief in the incessant crises of *Gone with the Wind*. Their contemporary experimenter in southern literary modernism, Eudora Welty,

examined the history and myth of her own South in the critical and
explorative manner of Faulkner, Tate, and Mitchell, but also sought to
find her own distinct perspective. Like Mitchell, Welty determined to
provide in her fictions the details and meanings inherent to southern
women's experience, and she did so with a sharply penetrating eye for
ambivalence and loss within the lives of southern women. There Welty
found her own unique strategy of the comic. For Welty insisted on
seeing every side of her women's history of the South: old women,
young women, black women, white women, poor women, rich
women, women sinned against, and women sinning. If Welty provided
no quintessential images of southern women, she offered them in infinite and humorous variety and with a degree of detachment and so-
phistication no other southern literary modernist could match.

Welty's portraits of southern women do parallel Mitchell's characters
in *Gone with the Wind,* but Welty's women are perceived amid endless
incongruities that create humor for Welty, whereas Mitchell envisioned
terror. It would seem that Welty's sense of the past was gathered and
recovered in an atmosphere of warmth and exuberance and so can be
seen from its comic as well as its serious side. Welty was only nine
years younger than Mitchell, and both women enjoyed a comfortably
middle-class upbringing in southern capital cities (Mitchell in Atlanta,
Welty in Jackson, Miss.), received excellent educations, and delighted
in their southern experience.[32] Welty's first longer fictions, *The Robber
Bridegroom* (1942) and *Delta Wedding* (1946), showed her concentration
on different aspects and interpretations of southern history and myth.
Although *The Robber Bridegroom* contained the local history of the
Natchez Trace, regional legends and tales, and a fantastic vision of the
perils of southern womanhood, it was also very funny. It was *Delta
Wedding,* Welty's second longer fiction, that most closely paralleled
Mitchell's *Gone with the Wind.* The interpenetrations between the two
works are so fascinating that it seems as if Welty's *Delta Wedding* was
written by a younger sister of Mitchell's who knew the old surviving
Civil War belles of *Gone with the Wind* and remembered them with the
detachment and humor created by a distance of fifty years or more.

Set on a plantation during the early years of this century, *Delta
Wedding* captured a version of the southern past and placed it within
the context of the twentieth century through the comic strategy of
vacillation between attitudes and experiences of past and present.
Welty perceived those vacillations as frequently so various as to provoke
laughter through sheer incongruity. Through Welty's journey into her

own history, her aesthetic control, like her southern modernist contemporaries, was expressive and confident. Welty created her own vision through a design of scene as a means of seeing the South: "The land was perfectly flat and level but it shimmered like the wings of a lighted dragonfly. It seem strummed, as though it were an instrument and something had touched it."[33] Here at the beginning of *Delta Wedding* Welty conveyed her aesthetic purpose and her radiant perspective. Hers would not be the South of Faulkner's complex and troubled hearts, the South of Tate's symbols of memory, or the South of Mitchell's women who survive. Welty's South was a land to be played with so that its seriousness would be tempered and tuned with comic irony and cunning strategy.

Delta Wedding begins on 10 September 1923, more than fifty years after the Civil War and Reconstruction blighted and, seemingly, altered southern experience, but for Welty time and wars signify little in a world of enduring family meanings. Welty chose the year 1923 deliberately because those who remembered the Civil War and its aftermath were still alive, and the period of the early 1920s was singularly uneventful on the Delta. In an interview, Welty observed that she wished to "concentrate on the people without any undue outside influences; I wanted to write a story that showed the solidity of this family and the life that went on on a small scale in a world of its own."[34] This world had been shaped by the Civil War, and the impact of that war was still felt amid the "solidity" of family. But it would be the people themselves who would challenge Welty's imagination, not the outside influences of disruption and violence. Welty's "family" would provide the focus, not a single central intelligence like Scarlett O'Hara, and the internal affairs of that family would provide more than enough turbulence, in Welty's view, so that the old war of the past would appear distant and quaintly calm by comparison.

What connected *Delta Wedding* so curiously to *Gone with the Wind*, then, was not the method of characterization nor the problem of theme, but the parallels of history and the possibilities of aesthetic consciousness revealed for both Welty and for Mitchell. Shellmound, the most important house on the Fairchild plantation, is inhabited by two old Civil War widows, the great-aunts of the family, Shannon and Mac. One might well imagine Scarlett, fifty years after Rhett's most determined desertion, and Melanie, resurrected as Scarlett wished so profoundly, living out their old age on a plantation filled with the children they fought so hard to protect. In *Delta Wedding* Shannon and

Mac had been left to mother and sustain eight children, the oldest of
whom was only twelve, when their brother James was killed in a duel
and his wife, Laura Allen, died of grief, and yet the two old women
who adopted this brood in their middle age had no trouble taking on
the orphans and are prepared to look after other children should the
need arise. By the early 1920s, Aunt Shannon's mind slips back and
forth through time as she talks with all the Fairchilds, whether alive
or dead, of her memory and her experience. In that she resembles her
counterpart in *Gone with the Wind,* for Scarlett begins having conver-
sations with the past during the Civil War and continues to find comfort in communicating with the past. Tales from the past bring solace
to the family at Fairchild, and symbols of that Civil War history bring
illumination to those who followed in time.

Both Welty and Mitchell communicate the meanings of the Civil
War through the experience of women. Those meanings inform women
in the twentieth century of the possibilities of their history and of the
responsibilities of their future by speaking to them of the past. For
example, Mitchell wrote in 1937 that *Gone with the Wind* was designed
to describe how "another world blew up under the unsuspecting feet
of our grandparents," and yet they found the means to survive. In her
novel Mitchell "looked back" on that time and found "that the same
qualities of courage are needed when, at any period of history, a world
turns over. And the same qualities of gentleness and idealism are
needed too."[35] For Mitchell there was no gender of courage or idealism
or gentleness; women and men displayed the capacity to meet a world
blowing up under their feet. For Welty that past was muted and transformed by humor and irony, but its significance was not entirely lost.
When the bride of *Delta Wedding* is asked to choose a family heirloom
for one of her wedding presents, she selects a flower bowl, but receives
instead a night-light that kept Civil War wives and widows, like Aunt
Shannon and Aunt Mac, company during their long—in some cases,
endless—wait for their husbands' return. When lit, the lamp heats
water for tea in the middle of the night and also reveals through its
decorated shade a picture of a little town of trees, towers, people,
houses, and a bridge. But through the shade a red glow permeates the
town, and so it seems that it is all on fire. The flickering of the candle
reveals ever so subtly the motion of flames in the town in this horrific
scene meant to bring comfort to lonely women. The fire in the night-
light, which captures, in a woman's symbol the terror of the fire in
Atlanta set by Sherman and fires all over the South that terrified civil-

ian populations, becomes an emblem of the old order nearly rent asunder at the same time as it functions as a gift of security and family to a younger generation of women who might otherwise forget their grandmothers' courage.

Delta Wedding was not designed to re-create the Old South as *Gone with the Wind* had been intended, and Welty's suggestive symbols from the past elicit humor—the bride, Dabney, did *not* ask for the Civil War night-light; it was imposed upon her—and with subtle intensities of meaning. Welty shared with her contemporary southern literary modernists the revelation of history and consciousness through the means of the artist's unique vision of place. Each of these writers experimented with language and form in order to design their own southern worlds. Faulkner's "postage stamp" of Yoknapatawpha, Tate's Pleasant Hill, Mitchell's Tara and her Atlanta, and Welty's Fairchild plantation with its Shellmound, Grove, and Marmion each embody their creators' intimacy with an imaginative landscape of their own making. Theirs was a South of the mind, a territory whose patterns of life and whose experience of history might vary from region to region—the "big woods" of Mississippi, the hills of Virginia, the North Georgia countryside and new capital, or the Mississippi River delta—but whose essential character would suffuse all their writings. Welty provided the clearest definition of this phenomenon in southern literary modernism: "Place absorbs our earliest notice and attention, it bestows on us our original awareness, and our critical powers spring up from the study of it and the growth of experience inside it."[36] The history and myth of the old plantation, the connections and symbols of family, the need for and the difficulty of communicating the past to new generations, the demand that the South change and come to prosper again on northern terms formed the crucial resources of southern literary modernism. Each writer made "a rug on the same loom," as Faulkner explained in *Absalom, Absalom!,* and the effort to weave unique patterns in that rug resulted in the extraordinary art of southern literary modernism. Margaret Mitchell employed those resources of history and family and aesthetic consciousness to devise her own pattern in the rug, her own version of past and of place.

Chapter Six

Text into Film:
The Making and Unmaking of
Gone with the Wind

To be frank, I do not care who they put in it or where they film it.
—Margaret Mitchell[1]

Margaret Mitchell's concern with language and literature demonstrated her familiarity with their contemporary literary artists and her understanding of the social and moral dimensions of history. But the making of her text into a popular film did not engage her interest. In a letter to Sidney Howard, the prizewinning playwright and initial author of the screenplay of *Gone with the Wind,* Mitchell wrote that she "would have nothing whatsoever to do with the picture" and that she did "not care who they put in it or where they [filmed] it"; her only concern was to stay as far away as possible from the filmmaking process. Mitchell repeatedly wrote that she had "told everybody simply that 'I know nothing about it and I have nothing to do with it' but often people think I am not telling the truth about matters like this (they just can't believe I know as little about the movie as I do), and probably I will be credited with having said a lot of things that never entered my mind." The filming of her novel merely increased the pressures of fame Mitchell had endured so ambivalently after the book's publication in 1936 and its tenure on the best-seller lists, and winning the Pulitzer Prize in 1937. She wrote, "this coming year [1939] may be even harder on us than 1936 was."[2]

The characteristic disclaimers Mitchell issued concerning the film actually echoed her depreciations of the success of the novel itself. Yet Mitchell, for all her self-deprecations and public disavowals of influence, did seek to affect subtly the making of the movie and did comprehend that by remaining publicly aloof she would possess greater impact and receive less criticism than if she initiated any overt efforts of her own. Mitchell's psychological distance from the film project became a public relations coup. For the film sold books, literally millions more, whenever it was released and "re-released." And the more Mitchell remained remote from the decision-making processes surrounding the film, the more attractive and appealing she became, particularly in contrast to David Selznick, the producer of the movie, who generated from Hollywood chaotic and overwhelming publicity. As always, Mitchell sought to gain and hold some form of control over the "ordeal" that *Gone with the Wind* created for her.[3]

When Macmillan organized the complex elements of the initial publication of *Gone with the Wind* in the spring of 1936, a number of movie companies became interested in the book from agents who believed the gossip circling the publications industry that the story had motion picture possibilities. Katherine Brown, Selznick's New York representative, sent a synopsis of the work and a copy of the novel itself to Selznick with the message, "I know that after you read the book you will drop everything and buy it."[4] Brown had received an advance copy in the middle of May, more than a month prior to the formal date of publication on 30 June 1936 from Macmillan. By 21 May 1936, Harold Latham of Macmillan wrote to Mitchell to ask her if she wished Macmillan to assume the role of agent "in connection with the possible motion picture sale." Mitchell agreed to Latham's suggestion, and on the same date as the letter requesting that Macmillan take on the responsibility of a potential film, Mitchell also received a $5,000 check as advance payment for future royalties.[5] On 29 July Mitchell, accompanied by Stephens Mitchell acting as her attorney, took an overnight train to New York in order to clarify and respond to the possible film offer. Mitchell wrote to Herschel Brickell toward the end of July with asperity: "I will stay in New York no longer than is necessary for me and brother Steve to clear up this damned moving picture contract. . . . I will lose my mind certainly if this thing isn't settled soon. Just now I don't care which way it is settled."[6] Here Mitchell revealed her ambivalence: On the one hand, she struggled over control of her novel and sought to influence the movie sale in her interest, but on the other hand, she insisted she did not want actually to care about the project. Much later, Mitchell's brother would attempt to clarify his sister's divided feelings: "Margaret wanted to go on and finish the matter. She did not wish to say that Macmillan had not done its best; she saw that no one (at least at that time only four weeks after the official publication of the novel) would offer more. It is difficult to realize it now, but $50,000 was a lot of money—the equivalent in the 1960s of

$200,000. . . . She did not want the worries which Hollywood could bring to her. She would not bother them, and they should not bother her."[7] Despite the Mitchells' exasperation over Macmillan's handling of the sale—they simply turned it over to a literary agent, Annie Laurie Williams, rather than assuming direct responsibility for Mitchell's own interests—they did not wish to alienate the firm from which they would gain much more than $50,000. Whatever Macmillan determined, whatever Selznick designed, Mitchell was as she wrote, "a hostage to the fortune" they created out of her work of art.[8]

For Mitchell, the "price of fame" was very high. She became "an international businesswoman specializing in copyright procedure and running a world wide enterprise from a small apartment" in Atlanta with the help of her husband and brother. The film contract devised by Selznick became the catalyst to the Mitchell family enterprise called "Gone with the Wind." By 5 August 1936 Mitchell, her husband, and her brother began to question the "thought that the publishers' interest marched exactly, or nearly so, with theirs."[9] The Mitchell family requested that Macmillan relieve them of the clerical and legal dilemma imposed by contractual and copyright obligations, and Macmillan refused outright. All further questions of rights were placed in Mitchell's hands, including all rights to foreign translations. The novel and the subsequent film took off on their own and took Mitchell with it.[10]

For Macmillan the sale of the film rights to David Selznick became a source of extraordinary free advertising. The sales of *Gone with the Wind* could scarcely even be counted, although the publisher sought to quantify its success as a means of stimulating even more success; when the millionth copy was sold in December 1936, the publicity department of Macmillan put out posters on American Express vans with the slogan "One million Americans can't be wrong—Read *Gone With the Wind*."[11] Mitchell's reaction was to write to Harold Latham at Macmillan to express her hope that she would be off the best-seller lists soon. Finis Farr sagely observed in the family-authorized biography of Mitchell that this "may be the only case on record in which an author hopefully asked a publisher if sales might not be coming down."[12] Her publisher could not oblige her request for falling sales. By the end of 1936 Mitchell had received more than $150,000 in royalties, and that would prove to be only the beginning of a flow of cash from the Macmillan Co. to the Mitchell account.[13]

Although Mitchell received a comparatively small sum in retrospect for the film rights to her novel, she was able to free herself from the actual burdens of drafting a screenplay or making creative decisions. She did insist that Wilbur Kurtz and Susan Myrick, both authorities on southern customs, be hired by Selznick to provide technical advice and dialect coaching. Mitchell's essential role in the making of the movie of *Gone with the Wind* was to cope gracefully with the "ordeal" of "attending the premiere" of the film in Atlanta. She did so, but even in her curtain speech she reminded her audience of the strain imposed by success. Mitchell observed, "Nobody needs to be told the value of friendship and consideration shown to one in adversity. But from my heart I tell you that its value can be greater to one who has experienced the incredible success I have." And her husband felt the need to press the point further in response to a question posed by a radio announcer: "Aren't you proud of your wife?" Marsh replied, "I was proud of her long before she wrote a book."[14] For Mitchell and for her husband, the film, like the publication of the novel, was one more "incredible success" to be endured carefully.

What Mitchell had to endure was a film that broke all financial records in the course of its continuing success. The public's interest in the Selznick film version was stimulated by the national search Selznick led to discover actors for the key roles. Selznick's *Gone with the Wind,* even more than D. W. Griffith's *Birth of a Nation* (1915), became the most popular American film of its time. Griffith's film was based on Thomas Dixon's *The Clansman* (1905), and both film and novel were designed to explain how the "wicked, cruel and causeless rebellion," as the Civil War is described, "was the one inevitable thing in our growth from a loose group of sovereign states to a United Nation."[15] Mitchell's text, although it shared a common subject matter with Dixon's novel, did not seek to politicize the past or romanticize the South. Mitchell sought to explore the experience of one southern woman's quest for survival in a world of ambiguities and cruelties she could not understand. Mitchell's novel was not portrayed with accuracy or even much understanding in the film version. Unlike the clear-cut simplicity and overt didacticism of Dixon's tale, the novel *Gone with the Wind* could not be translated neatly into the images that suffuse the silent and powerful *Birth of a Nation*. In lieu of representing much of the meaning of Mitchell's text, Selznick dramatized the "land of cavaliers and cotton fields," as the prologue to the film explains, and replicated the fire in Atlanta and other details with elaborate accuracy.[16] The ambivalence and incomprehension so essential to Scarlett's character was softened in the film version; the relationship between

Scarlett and Melanie was trivialized into a jealous quarrel that Melanie was incapable of understanding; and the subtleties of Mitchell's conclusion were subverted into an almost humorous power struggle between Scarlett and Rhett. The film Selznick made was his own creation, not Mitchell's.

As David Selznick prepared to produce his own *Gone with the Wind,* he emphasized certain political factors he desired Sidney Howard to explore. Selznick wrote, "I, for one, have no desire to produce an anti-Negro film either. In our picture I think we have to be awfully careful that the Negroes come out decidedly on the right side of the ledger. . . . I personally feel quite strongly that we should cut out the Klan entirely" or the film "might come out as an unintentional advertisement for intolerant societies in these fascist-ridden times."[17] Selznick's desire to reshape the novel into a film devoid of complexity of ideas was perhaps natural. He drew portraits of blacks, such as Hattie McDaniel's Oscar-winning performance as "Mammy," that were stronger and less sterotypical than in the novel; in Butterfly McQueen's "Prissy" there was a perfectly controlled comic element in the film quite lacking in the novel. These actors were enabled to present Negro characters that "came out decidedly on the right side of the ledger," at least in Selznick's terms, although they also represented only "modest revisions of ancient stereotypes."[18] Certainly, Selznick sought not to alienate any of his constituencies—southern whites, northerners, foreign audiences, and blacks. By reducing the significance of the Klan and by also ignoring Mitchell's portrayal of free and newly assertive blacks during Reconstruction, Selznick eliminated a good deal of the complex representation of women's vulnerability and their problems of survival in the postwar South. For white women the fear of rape "served to keep a subordinate group in a state of anxiety and fear" and prevented assertive women, like Scarlett, from challenging traditional patterns of behavior.[19] Selznick sought to reconstruct the rape scene in *Gone with the Wind* by making the black character "little more than a spectator."[20] Mitchell's effort to reveal Scarlett as threatened and vulnerable to a male-created and male-dominated world of violence is subverted in the scene. Her fear and anxiety as well as her struggle and achievement are reduced in her film representation. She is more a spoiled brat who is too beautiful for her own good in Selznick's design and less the survivor whose fear-filled demands for her self and those she seeks to protect make her unhappy and uncomprehending in Mitchell's sympathetic yet ambivalent vision.

Selznick's cinematic view of Scarlett O'Hara and her southern experience was his own; his South was "an invented place, where imagined ideals were invoked as a structure for reality" even when that reality was questioned by the very text from which Selznick worked.[21] The film sought to preserve "a defensive, pristine, and idealistic view" that affected the characterization of plantation life so that it appeared quite "unblemished by ugly past realities still too immediate for unbiased scrutiny."[22] In Mitchell's fictional account of one woman's experience of precisely those "ugly past realities" she sought to reveal ambiguities Selznick ignored.

Selznick's re-creation of Mitchell's story was striking in its capacity to provide the viewer with access to long-past events: the Civil War and Reconstruction.[23] The film was eagerly awaited by millions of Americans who would not read Mitchell's book. A December 1939 Gallup poll reported that 56.5 million people planned to see the film of *Gone with the Wind*.[24] In his *The Celluloid South*, Edward Campbell observed that Selznick's *Gone with the Wind* became a kind of national epic that met psychic needs of Southerners to idealize their experience and that spoke to Northerners' desire to understand the past. The simplicity of Selznick's presentation allowed Southerners and Northerners alike to enjoy his portrait of the Old South with little hesitation or much consciousness of the divided and irresolvable realities Mitchell sought to reveal.[25]

At first, Mitchell was neither disquieted by Selznick's publicity techniques nor disturbed by the "true southern epic" she believed he sought to create. Her "own noncommittal but pleasant attitude" toward the making of *Gone with the Wind* into film became more and more detached, although she recognized many of the problems with the Selznick production. Yet as she wrote to Susan Myrick, one of the authorities on southern customs recommended by Mitchell and hired by Selznick, "I have always been one to take 'the long view.' Moreover, for nearly three years I've had a box seat with an excellent view of the reactions of the public mind, especially the southern mind. It sometimes seems to me that *Gone with the Wind* is not my book any longer." By assuming a "long view" of the movie, Mitchell sought to protect herself as much as possible. Yet even "after more than two years of having my life upset by this movie," Mitchell found herself in the awkward position of having no real authority at all: "I am desperately tired of standing in the middle ground between the movie folks and the public."[26] Neither would let her alone, and neither held any real pleasure or comfort for her.

In fact, Mitchell felt she was in an impossible circumstance created by the Selznick publicity machine, and she actually threatened legal action against the producer for misrepresenting her opinions or her name in any manner. Certainly, Selznick's lack of understanding had annoyed Mitchell, for she wrote, "Mr. S. is not a Southerner, of course, and knows practically nothing of our psychology."[27] But her concern over Selznick's tactics grew as he continued to exploit her renown for his own purposes. Mitchell wrote to him with explicit concern: "What I am asking is that your publicity leave me in my position as author and not attempt to drag me into the position of co-producer. . . . I am entitled to ask that your Publicity Department show me the consideration of not misrepresenting my connection with the film." But Mitchell's conviction was that she was a victim of Selznick's operations: "Ever since the summer of 1936," she wrote on 13 March 1939, while her book was being filmed, "your film has been a subject of public controversy, and, for no good reason at all, I have been caught in the storm center of the controversy." Because Selznick sought to exploit the extraordinarily ordinary nature of this Atlanta housewife turned best-selling author into a publicity device to enhance the attention paid to his film, Mitchell felt he had "created a problem for me many times greater than any of my other problems as the author of *Gone with the Wind*." She *had* no control: "My connection with the motion picture ended on 30 July 1936 when I signed the contract selling you the film rights."[28]

The Selznick version of *Gone with the Wind* became a kind of lightning rod to Mitchell's conception of herself as author. The film absorbed considerable amounts of energy and trouble, but it also focused problems in the "storm center" of Mitchell's experience in a highly visible and frightening manner. Mitchell's fear of Selznick's power became so great that she sought to threaten him legally: "If I am to be rewarded for my courtesy by being placed in a false position and having my name misused, I will be forced to take steps of my own to make my position clear to the public."[29] Selznick responded with reassurance that he had "again cautioned MGM not to misuse" Mitchell or her name in any way.[30] What was so remarkable about the conflict Mitchell perceived in Selznick's highly successful production efforts was that Mitchell remained so sensitive to the issue of publicity at all. After all, as she herself repeated again and again, she no longer possessed control over the film rights so that whatever occurred could not be her responsibility. Any film version would create controversy, and any film version would create royalties. Mitchell was bound to find her share in the profits of sales of her novel to be greatly enlarged by the very publicity she deplored so vehemently.

By February 1940 the film had already been shown to ten million people; by June of that year, when the first run had been completed, more than twenty-five million had viewed it. The Hollywood version was not Mitchell's novel. Yet, as Mitchell observed, "We southerners could write the truth about the antebellum South, its few slaveholders, its yeomen farmers, its rambling, comfortable houses just fifty years away from log cabins, until Gabriel blows his trumpet—and everyone would go on believing in the Hollywood version. The sad part is that many Southerners believe this myth even more ardently than Northerners."[31] Selznick's film plagued Mitchell for years to come: after the film had won ten Academy Awards and many other critics' awards and brought tremendous wealth to its producer, Mitchell faced only increased mail and outrageous rumor. For example, Selznick contended after the film had been produced that he would have been willing to pay $250,000 for the film rights rather than the $50,000 Mitchell had received. Selznick did offer $50,000 in additional payment in 1942, and, in fact, Mitchell's novel royalties were enlarged as sales of books increased during each run of the film. She would struggle with rumors of alcoholism, plagiarism, potential sequels, insanity, eccentricity, and sheer stupidity until her death in 1949.[32]

After the first run of Selznick's film, Mitchell sought to resume something of a private life. But, in 1941, Selznick, who hoped to capitalize on the success of his film version, sought to create a musical version for the Broadway stage and desired to conduct still another national talent search for the principal actors. After months of negotiations, Mitchell asked her husband to reject the project. Marsh wrote, "Peggy just doesn't feel like making the trade on the basis he has proposed. What you [Kay Brown, Selznick's New York representative] said about a talent search wasn't the only reason for the rejection of the offer but it was one reason, and I am going to make one more effort to explain our position. . . . No amount of money would ever induce Peggy to go through another experience like the one she was subjected to by the talent search for the movie. It was a fine buildup for the movie; it got publicity for the movie which you might not have gotten otherwise, but it was hell on earth for Peggy. I doubt that Mr. Selznick has even gotten the faintest conception of what it did to Peggy."[33] The point John Marsh so strongly articulated to Brown and especially to Selznick was that no one could really conceive Mitchell's reaction to her fame and success and that no one should ask her to be "subjected to" another round.

Margaret Mitchell never entirely recovered from the overdose of renown. It was fame's devastating consequences that John Marsh believed prevented his wife from further fiction writing. Marsh observed that the pressure of fame "uses up innumerable hours of time, and time is the only working capital of an author, by still further postponing the time when she can begin writing again, as she ardently wishes to do." The "hell on earth" Selznick had wrought with his award-winning film of her novel prevented Mitchell from accomplishing her longed-for "wish" to write another novel or from ever having a normal life again.

Other reasons also precluded Mitchell from returning to fiction writing: she cared for her father during his lingering illness and death on 17 June 1944, and she devoted vast time and financial resources to the Red Cross and the United Service Organizations during World War II, just as she and her mother had performed such service during World War I. A few months after World War II ended, Mitchell and her husband visited the sea islands of Georgia during Christmas of 1945; there Marsh suffered a serious heart attack, was hospitalized for several months, and returned home for his long recovery under his wife's care. Time, "the only working capital of an author," was in short supply, as Mitchell struggled to care for her husband and manage the Gone with the Wind business without his help.[34] If Mitchell possessed any ardent wish to continue writing novels, her desire could not be fulfilled. Her husband had propelled her into writing *Gone with the Wind,* had supported her through the "hell on earth" the film version of the novel had created for them both, and now he required her to sustain him as he had so sensitively nurtured her through the ordeals of the past.

Conclusion

She had said something to her people, and they had answered.

—Stephens Mitchell[1]

The significance of Margaret Mitchell's career was its record of a woman whose life and work were ordered and traditional yet paradoxically marked by experimentation and exploration. Her vision was ambivalent; she sought to challenge traditional expectations at the same time that she cultivated the past as a source of stability and sustenance. Mitchell was not an easy person to understand, and her single novel does not have an easy affiliation by which it could be known in the literary canon. For Mitchell and her southern modernist contemporaries, history proved such a forceful presence that critical categories and polemical commonalities seemed less important than the discovery of unique forms and patterns within the meaning and memory of the past. Mitchell's own effort in *Gone with the Wind* was to take the measure of America itself through the north Georgia manners and morals of a young woman and to see within the secrets of her ambivalent heroine the patterns of social destruction and social stability that inform the country as a whole.

Mitchell sought a vision of America embattled and yet surviving, and she saw in the individual assertion of a woman neither beautiful nor good a world of excitement and possibility as well as frustration and death. It is no wonder that Mitchell's novel was popular: she created a romanticized and feminized encounter with history in which the intimate vicarious possibility of knowing that history from within, of seeing that experience through the vividly reshaped detail of Mitchell's research, cannot be underestimated.

In his "Ode to the Confederate Dead" Allen Tate compressed the subtle meanings of southern experience with history in an image of an individual waiting "for the angry resolution / of those desires that should be yours tomorrow" and of knowing "the unimportant shrift of death" and of praising "the vision" that memory endows. In her own way Mitchell was reacting to the crisis of individualism that preoccupied male explorations of southern experience with history, but Mitchell sought in the "angry resolution of those desires that should be yours tomorrow" the meaning of a woman who was a victim, not a visionary. Tate's panegyric to "the vision" of "those who fall" and of those who wait in "mute speculation" became a means by which the artist could hold off the horror of historical chaos and private moral confusion through the complex, measured meaning of the ode.[2] Tate perceived his consolation, his "knowledge carried to the heart," in the grave he shared with his confederate dead. For Mitchell, the comfort of that grave would not seem so sure. Her vision of confederate dead would demand the recognition of confederate widows and confederate orphans, and she wrote their story in *Gone with the Wind*. Mitchell pondered and explored the idea of an individual waiting for "the angry resolution of those desires that should be yours tomorrow" through the character of Scarlett, but Mitchell could not imagine resolution or knowledge or comfort. Only a kind of sturdy survival instinct and the will to avoid the grave and circumvent the undesirable propelled Scarlett at the end of *Gone with the Wind*. Mitchell believed that Scarlett's experience with southern history stood in need of expression. In love, in avarice, in labor, in family, in survival, Mitchell uttered Scarlett's secrets, and in so doing she fascinated her reading public with a private world of southern history.

The very intimacy that suffused *Gone with the Wind* and attracted uncounted readers nearly overwhelmed the woman who told Scarlett's secrets to the world. Mitchell's detailed observation of manners and social milieu were combined with a commanding perception of the underlying human patterns of experience that lie beneath them. And in the explosion of the false and the pompous, even the silliness and self-deception of her heroine, Mitchell's novel revealed a sustaining web of feelings that had been repressed. Having given such feelings their due—some might say their overdue—Mitchell became, in effect, their custodian. The sympathetic detachment Mitchell projected as the narrator of *Gone with the Wind* and as the author of a multitude of letters to readers in the decade and half following publication of her novel was countered by the immediacies of film production and personal confrontation that were thrust at her. The writing of a enormously popular book might be profitable, but it was also unpalatable. At least for Mitchell, the vulnerability such an action created in her life was overwhelming, and it prevented her from writing other books: "To tell the hideous truth," she wrote to an intimate in 1938, "I have never once in my life felt a compulsion to write anything. The exact opposite has been my problem. I loathe writing and will go to any lengths to keep from writing. Having a definite antipathy for putting words on paper, the only reason I ever wrote any was because I had nothing to do at that particular time and, having started something, was goaded on by the Puritanical adage that one should finish what one had begun. John's large shoe placed on the metaphorical seat of the pants of my soul accelerated some of my efforts."[3] Mitchell's image of being kicked into writing, of being so bored that "something," anything, even writing, was better than "nothing to do" showed her delightful will to make herself a detached, slightly ironic, witness to her own career. She may have been the only person capable of putting pants on her soul, just as she was the only person capable of creating an irrepressible Scarlett woman. Individual assertion of energy and will created Scarlett and expressed her personal anarchism, but it cost the creator of such secret exposures of power and force in women too much in Mitchell's estimation: "Seeing the enormous amount of work and worry I have brought on my family and myself, I would think several times before really trying to publish a book."[4] Mitchell was critical of her effort, for she was as quick to catch the essence of the American publishing industry—exploitation of mass appeal—as she was to capture the rugged individualism of Scarlett O'Hara as a traditional, although female, American antiheroine in quest of selfhood in a world of threat.

Mitchell knew that "to a professional writer it is valuable to be known," but she sought to control the terms of being "known" for the rest of her life after the publication of *Gone with the Wind*. The threat imposed by public exposure proved more than she could withstand. Whatever the cost of self-exposure, Mitchell wrote, "I have always felt that people who would not fight for what they had deserved to lose it. So, I intend to keep on fighting."[5] She, like the antiheroine she designed, was a fighter, a survivor of extraordinary resilience and energy. This woman with "a passionate desire for personal privacy" was able to achieve a public success by revealing the "beauty and poetry in the Georgia voice and the Georgia way of expressing things," and in so doing created a novel that would "be simple enough" in her own words, "for a child of five to understand."[6] That deliberate simplicity, like Mitchell's determined self-protectiveness, would ensure the world's fascination. The ambivalence she expressed—her will to self-assertion and her vulnerability—were projected on her heroine, Scarlett. Unique and isolated, Mitchell's Scarlett has few resources to challenge male power, and she survives an experience of broken promises, thwarted expectations, and endless demands. Yet Mitchell's Scarlett, unlike Mitchell herself, possesses no stable, supportive, and stimulating husband. Scarlett enjoys no loving brother like Stephens, who would write in his memoir of his sister, "I cannot give you her bad points, for to me she had none."[7] Margaret Mitchell faced the demands and problems of too much success for many years, and she survived them with grace, if not a little frustration, because she was loved and understood. Her death, like much of her life, was in the public domain. She was hit by an automobile in Atlanta and died on the morning of 16 August 1949. Many years of Mitchell's life had been lived as a professional writer, and after her funeral her brother recorded that at the cemetery "there was a crowd there for two or three days. She had said something to her people and they had answered."[8]

Mitchell's work survives just as she had predicted Scarlett would endure "to another day" (GW, 1037). She had learned from her own errors, from her lost opportunities, and from her first ruined marriage, to cherish family, to achieve success, and to appreciate her second husband. Mitchell's ambivalence also allowed her to create a female character who defies proprieties, pioneers a publicly successful role for herself, and yet still insists on her correct social position within the genteel world of Atlanta. Scarlett O'Hara's ambivalence about what she really wants is mirrored still in women's ambivalence in the late twentieth century.

Too much success, like too much failure, must, from Mitchell's point of view, be understood, not merely accepted or deplored. The capacity to understand and the ability to communicate were acts of survival and triumph for Mitchell—ways of coping with disaster in a world of threat. Mitchell's work of art and her creation of herself reflect her will to understand; in *Gone with the Wind* she provided a map of the ways to comprehend men and men's power. Margaret Mitchell's vision of Scarlett O'Hara gazing out after Rhett Butler's departure provided both the beginning and the ending of her novel: "She wondered forlornly if she had ever really understood anyone in the world" (GW, 1036). That would never stop Mitchell from trying.

Notes and References

Preface

1. "Margaret Mitchell," *Wilson Quarterly* 11 (September 1936): 12.
2. See the sales figures included in Susan Geary's "The Domestic Novel as a Commercial Commodity," *Bibliographical Society of America* (July 1976): 369–70, for other examples of the steady and then astounding increase in book sales in the first half of the nineteenth century.
3. A number of scholars have explored this period as one of democratization and feminization in American culture; see especially Henry Nash Smith, *Democracy and the Novel* (New York: Oxford University Press, 1978); Ann Douglas, *The Feminization of American Culture* (New York: Knopf, 1977); Nina Baym, *Women's Fiction: A Guide to Novels by and about Women, 1820–1870* (Ithaca, N.Y.: Cornell University Press, 1978); and Jane Tompkins, *Sensational Designs: The Cultural Work of American Fiction, 1790–1860* (New York: Oxford University Press, 1985).
4. For a careful analysis of Stowe's fiction, see Alice Crozier's *The Novels of Harriet Beecher Stowe* (New York: Oxford University Press, 1969).
5. Harriet Beecher Stowe, *Uncle Tom's Cabin*, ed. Kenneth Lynn (Cambridge: Harvard University Press, 1962), 456–57; *Gone with the Wind* (New York: Macmillan, 1936), 1015; hereafter cited in the text as *GW*.

Chapter One

1. Finis Farr (and Stephens Mitchell), *Margaret Mitchell of Atlanta: The Author of "Gone with the Wind"* (New York: Morrow, 1965). Farr writes that the "foundation of this book is in the papers of the Margaret Mitchell Marsh Estate and in an unpublished memoir by Stephens Mitchell." The copyright to *Margaret Mitchell of Atlanta: The Author of "Gone with the Wind"* is held by both Finis Farr and Stephens Mitchell. In this collaborative family biography Farr quotes liberally from Stephens Mitchell's unpublished memoir. It is Stephens Mitchell's contention that Margaret's childhood was "absolutely secure," although he provides important evidence of accidents, fire, financial disaster, war-time pessimism, and lack of "social success" in Atlanta.
2. Margaret Mitchell to Julia Collier Harris, 28 April 1936, *Margaret Mitchell's "Gone with the Wind" Letters, 1936–1949*, ed. Richard Harwell (New York: Macmillan, 1976), 16–18.
3. An excellent history of Reconstruction Georgia is included in N. Bartley's *The Creation of Modern Georgia* (Athens: The University of Georgia Press, 1983), 45–74.

4. Willard Range, the historian of the Georgia agricultural economy, defines the postbellum period as the "long Depression of 1865 to 1900." See his *A Century of Georgia Agriculture, 1865–1900* (Athens: University of Georgia Press, 1954), 107–22, for a careful analysis of the agricultural and economic crises in Georgia, particularly during the time of Margaret Mitchell's parents' youth.

5. Lee Soltow, *Men and Wealth in the United States, 1850–1870* (New Haven: Yale University Press, 1975), 92–101.

6. Charles Reagan Wilson, *Baptized in Blood: The Religion of the Lost Cause, 1865–1920* (Athens: University of Georgia Press, 1980), 1. See also Rollin G. Osterweis, *The Myth of the Lost Cause, 1865–1900* (Hamden, Connecticut: Archon, 1973).

7. See the research of Floyd Hunter into the history and development of the Atlanta elite in his *Community Power Structure: A Study of Decision Makers* (Chapel Hill: University of North Carolina Press, 1953) and *Community Power Succession: Atlanta's Policy-Makers Revisited* (Chapel Hill: University of North Carolina Press, 1980).

8. Farr (and Stephens Mitchell), *Margaret Mitchell of Atlanta*, 18–27.

9. Bartley, *The Creation of Modern Georgia*, 108–12.

10. Farr (and Stephens Mitchell), *Margaret Mitchell of Atlanta*, 19–20.

11. Ibid., 19.

12. Ibid., 27.

13. Ibid., 14, 31–34.

14. Margaret Mitchell to Henry Steele Commager, 10 July 1936, *Margaret Mitchell's "Gone with the Wind" Letters, 1936–1949*, 37–40.

15. Farr (and Stephens Mitchell), *Margaret Mitchell of Atlanta*, 30–35 and Anne Edwards, *Road to Tara: The Life of Margaret Mitchell* (New York: Dell, 1983), 15–45.

16. See, for example, the excellent chapter, "Progressivism and the End of an Era," in Bartley's *The Creation of Modern Georgia*, 147–78, and also, John Dittmer's *Black Georgia in the Progressive Era, 1900–1920* (Urbana: University of Illinois Press, 1977).

17. Hoke Smith was quoted by the *Atlanta Journal*, 10 October 1906, and his statement was cited by Bartley in his *The Creation of Modern Georgia*, 148–49, 227.

18. Margaret Mitchell's letter to Mrs. Sydney Howard was written in response to a series of articles in the *Atlantic Monthly* and was cited by Farr (and Stephens Mitchell) in *Margaret Mitchell of Atlanta*, 22–23.

19. The quotation was recorded in Stephens Mitchell's unpublished memoir and was included in Farr's (and Stephens Mitchell), *Margaret Mitchell of Atlanta*, 23.

20. Anne Firor Scott, *The Southern Lady: From Pedestal to Politics, 1830–1930* (Chicago: University of Chicago Press, 1970), 90.

21. Farr (and Stephens Mitchell), *Margaret Mitchell of Atlanta*, 35.

22. Ibid., 36.
23. Ibid., 38.
24. Ibid., 38.
25. Ibid., 38.
26. Ibid., 39.
27. Ibid., 39–40.
28. Ibid.
29. Ibid., 43.

Chapter Two

1. Farr (and Stephens Mitchell), *Margaret Mitchell of Atlanta,* 43–44.
2. Ibid., 44.
3. Ibid., 46.
4. Ibid., 46–47.
5. See Helen L. Horowitz, *Alma Mater: Design and Experience in Women's Colleges from Nineteenth Century Beginnings to the Nineteen Thirties* (New York: Knopf, 1984), 323–24; for a careful analysis of the significance of women's colleges in the lives of "prominent families" in American cities during the 1920s see pp. 283–84.
6. Farr (and Stephens Mitchell), *Margaret Mitchell of Atlanta,* 50.
7. Ibid., 50.
8. Ibid., 54
9. Ibid., 43.
10. Ibid., 52–55.
11. Ibid., 55.
12. Ibid., 56.
13. Ibid., 56–57.
14. Ibid., 57.
15. Ibid., 57.
16. See the remembrances of Medora and Angus Perkerson reprinted in *"Gone with the Wind" As Book and Film,* ed. Richard Harwell (Columbia: University of South Carolina Press, 1983), 39–45. Medora Perkerson recorded her sense of the relationship between Mitchell's newspaper career and the writing of *Gone with the Wind* in an article published 7 January 1945 in the *Atlanta Journal Sunday Magazine,* "When Margaret Mitchell was a Girl Reporter."
17. Farr (and Stephens Mitchell), *Margaret Mitchell of Atlanta,* 58–60.
18. See Mary Kelley's *Private Woman, Public Stage: Literary Domesticity in Nineteenth-Century America* (New York: Oxford, 1984) for a fascinating analysis of the "ambiguous positions" such socially prominent daughters of elite families found as they also made literary careers for themselves by becoming popular, commercially successful writers of fiction and nonfiction (111–12).
19. Farr (and Stephens Mitchell), *Margaret Mitchell of Atlanta,* 58–77.
20. Ibid., 18–19.

Chapter Three

1. Farr (and Stephens Mitchell), *Margaret Mitchell of Atlanta,* 59–60.

2. W. A. Swanberg, *Citizen Hearst* (New York: Scribner's, 1961), 90.

3. Michael Schudson in his classic study *Discovering the News: A Social History of American Newspapers* (New York: Basic, 1978) describes the important social changes responsible for the creation of the Sunday illustrated magazine (98–99). Schudson believes that "the practice of printing special Sunday editions with war news" during the Civil War "made it easier for papers to take the plunge into Sunday journalism" (99).

4. See the fine study by George Juergens, *Joseph Pulitzer and the New York World* (Princeton: Princeton University Press, 1966), for information on Pulitzer's experiments in Sunday illustrated magazines (56–57).

5. Schudson, *Discovering the News,* 99–101.

6. Farr (and Stephens Mitchell), *Margaret Mitchell of Atlanta,* 67.

7. Mitchell, "Old Roswell," *Atlanta Journal,* 10 June 1923. See a fuller treatment of the history of Roswell in Malcolm Bell, Jr.'s *Major Butler's Legacy: Five Generations of a Slave-Holding Family* (Athens: University of Georgia Press, 1987), which devotes several chapters to the career of Roswell King, Sr., who founded the town of Roswell just north of Atlanta in 1838 by luring families, like the Bullochs, from Georgia's mosquito-infested coastal lowlands. King had begun his career as a manager of a coastal Sea Island plantation owned by Pierce Butler, and in Roswell he sought to found a community in his own name and image.

8. Farr (and Stephens Mitchell), *Margaret Mitchell of Atlanta,* 69–70.

9. Ibid., 70–77.

10. See Mary Kelley's "No Happy Woman Writers" in her *Private Woman, Public Stage* for an analysis of the "peculiar circumstances" that allowed women to benefit from opportunities presented by the commercial publishing industry in the nineteenth and twentieth centuries (138–63).

11. Farr (and Stephens Mitchell), *Margaret Mitchell of Atlanta,* 57, 69.

12. Ibid., 77.

13. William O'Neill has written with both prescience and lucidity concerning the meaning of divorce within the intensely demanding family system in the Progressive era; in Mitchell's time, O'Neill writes, the social position of the American woman was not greatly different from what it was at the end of the nineteenth century when the Victorian family system had still demonstrated an astonishing durability. So much so that "when families become the center for social organization, their intimacy can become suffocating, their demands unbearable, and their expectations too high to be easily realizable. Divorce then becomes the safety value that makes the system workable" (*Divorce in the Progressive Era* [New Haven, Conn.: Yale University Press, 1967], viii, 6–7). Mitchell sought to make the system workable in her second marriage.

14. See Shelley Fisher Fishkin's *From Fact into Fiction: Journalism and Imaginative Writing in America* (Baltimore: Johns Hopkins University Press, 1985) for a useful exploration of the continuities and discontinuities in the journalism and fiction of five major American writers: Whitman, Mark Twain, Dreiser, Hemingway, and Dos Passos. Fishkin does not examine other authors, although she lists many, from John Greenleaf Whittier to John Hersey, in her introduction, nor does she consider the ramifications of her argument for women journalists, such as Stowe, Cather, Porter, Welty, and Mitchell herself (3, 7–9).

15. Farr (and Stephens Mitchell), *Margaret Mitchell of Atlanta,* 77.

16. Ibid., 78.

Chapter Four

1. Farr (and Stephens Mitchell), *Margaret Mitchell of Atlanta,* 84.

2. Ibid., 84.

3. Edmund Wilson, *Patriotic Gore: Studies in the Literature of the American Civil War* (New York: Oxford University Press, 1962), 438. Still the best and most sensitive source to Civil War literature of the South and the North. See also Paul Gaston's *The New South Creed: A Study in Southern Mythmaking* (New York: Knopf, 1970), 151–86.

4. During the Reconstruction era especially, a number of writers from both the South and the North began to explore Civil War materials in fiction. For examinations of these postbellum fictional designs, see Joyce Appleby's "Reconciliation and the Northern Novelist, 1865–1880," *Civil War History* 10 (June 1964): 117–29, and C. Vann Woodward's "A Southern Critique for the Gilded Age" in his *The Burden of Southern History* (Baton Rouge: Louisiana State University Press, 1960), 109–40.

5. See Douglas's *The Feminization of American Culture* for a fuller account of how such "decorous deviousness" could be employed to exert women's power of influence over men, 71. Douglas also examines the development of a "disestablishment" and reduction in the status of women from productive roles they played in earlier times to the status of consumers and demonstrators of men's wealth in the latter half of the nineteenth century. This consumerism is now a main basis of American culture, but for Mitchell, such passive, unproductive roles for women required questioning. In *Gone with the Wind,* the more productive roles of the past are embodied by Ellen O'Hara and her generation, and the consumers in transition are portrayed by Scarlett's contemporaries, especially her sister Suellen and her weaker, less capable female friends. Scarlett seeks a productive role and yet is continually punished for desiring an active, effective means of supporting her family and Ashley Wilkes. Only Melanie Wilkes appears able to understand and even to support Scarlett's efforts to support them both.

6. See Bertram Wyatt-Brown's "Woman in a Man's World: Role and Self Image" in the antebellum South in his *Southern Honor: Ethics and Behavior in the Old South* (New York: Oxford University Press, 1982) for a careful examination of the tense and competitive struggles between southern men and women. Wyatt-Brown sees that the conflict for women "had to be subterranean and devious, for men alone were given the privilege of expressing their feelings openly. Antagonisms grew out of the conflict, but also out of the misogyny that arose from male fear of female power" (226–53). *Southern Honor* also contains important analyses of how the "toughness between the soft exterior" of southern women served to reinforce family honor and courage and yet ensure at least outward submission to male will.

7. See Carroll Smith-Rosenberg's "The Female World of Love and Ritual: Relations between Women in Nineteenth-Century America," *Signs*, 1, no. 1 (Autumn 1975): 1–29, for a useful study of the intense love between women that constituted an integral part of social life in times when men were away at war. Single and widowed women, but also married women, maintained the primacy of their female friendships because they provided women with networks and ties of common interests and also of survival in times of difficulty.

8. Wyatt-Brown, *Southern Honor*, 234–35.

9. See Blanche Gelfant's "*Gone with the Wind* and The Impossibilities of Fiction" in her collection of essays *Women Writing in America: Voices in Collage* (Hanover, N.H.: University Press of New England, 1984) where she describes how the novel "makes our worst fears manageable, fears of war, rape, chaos, hunger, death" because "it also gratifies our most infantile wish, the one Scarlett expressed—that we get everything we want. . . . The reader's pleasure is a fulfillment of impossible desires" (171–201).

10. *Margaret Mitchell's "Gone with the Wind" Letters, 1936–1949*, 13–15. Harry Stillwell Edwards's review-essay of *Gone with the Wind* was included in his column "Coming Down My Creek" and appeared in the 14 June 1936 *Atlanta Journal*.

11. See Philip Fisher's *Hard Facts: Setting and Form in the American Novel* (New York: Oxford University Press, 1985), 14–16, for a careful analysis of how the historical novel develops into popular forms of fiction. Fisher cites the work of György Lukács as the key source on how the historical novel transforms notions of character by replacing moral individuality with a more historical and deterministic notion of type and typicality. See, especially, Lukács's *The Historical Novel*, trans. Hannah and Stanley Mitchell (Boston: Beacon Press, 1962), for other examples of how the historical novel imposes an event structure of action that miniaturizes the significant play of forces of a whole world of action into a comprehensible and, at times, even allegorical text.

12. *Margaret Mitchell's "Gone with the Wind" Letters, 1936–1949*, 15.

13. Philip Fisher, *Hard Facts,* 15.

14. Margaret Mitchell's radio interview with Medora Field Perkerson reprinted in the *Atlanta Journal Sunday Magazine* on 23 May 1937, 1–2.

15. Floyd C. Watkins, in his *"Gone with the Wind* as Vulgar Literature," *Southern Literary Journal* 2 (Spring 1970): 86–103, provides the clearest case for Mitchell's historical failures in her novel. Watkins may take Mitchell's historicism a bit more seriously than she or her readers have.

16. M. W. Jones recorded the essential contents of Margaret Mitchell's speech in Macon, Georgia, following the publication of *Gone with the Wind,* in an article entitled "Me and My Book," *Georgia Review* 16 (Summer 1962): 180–87. The quotation cited in the text came at the end of the speech when Mitchell informed the audience she would conclude on a "serious note" concerning the significance of her novel for southern writers, particularly in their relation to their northern readers and northern publishers (186).

17. Farr (and Stephens Mitchell), *Margaret Mitchell of Atlanta,* 29–30.

18. Ibid., 30.

19. For revealing insight on the problems of a "secret alliance" between Scarlett and Melanie, see especially Mary Kelley's "The Great Question of the Moral Life" in her *Private Woman, Public Stage,* 252–53; Smith-Rosenberg's "The Female World of Love and Ritual," 1–30; and Nancy Cott's *The Bonds of Womanhood* (New Haven, Conn.: Yale University Press, 1977), 160–96. These scholars explore the concept of a female world that encompasses particular values of courage under pressure and persistence in attachments to other women and children, if not to men. This female world also provides sustenance through rituals of childbirth, death, and widowhood, and friendship networks that offer intense, emotionally fulfilling contact between women.

20. Jones, "Me and My Book," 185.

21. See John G. Cawelti's *Adventure, Mystery, and Romance: Formula Stories as Art and Popular Culture* (Chicago: University of Chicago Press, 1976), especially 38–39, for a lucid analysis of the purposes of "moral fantasy" in popular fictions and romances.

22. Kay Mussell in the "History" chapter of her book *Women's Gothic and Romantic Fiction* (Westport, Conn.: Greenwood, 1981) places *Gone with the Wind* within the genre of antiromance because the protagonist, Scarlett, loses "her true love." Mussell does argue that "Melanie is a major character," but one who is the "diametrical opposite" of Scarlett not the "blindly passionate" lover of Scarlett that Mitchell designs (13–14).

23. See Anne Goodwin Jones's essay *"Gone with the Wind* and Others: Popular Fiction, 1920–1950" in *The History of Southern Literature* (Baton Rouge: Louisiana State University Press, 1985) for an interesting view on gender in the novel. Jones argues that Scarlett is a woman "for whom love is not the reward of her experience" (392); it is nostalgia for patriarchal safety. Jones's interpretation is a mildly feminist revision of traditional scholarship

on *Gone with the Wind*, which fails to consider Mitchell's development of the Scarlett-Melanie configuration amid the more conventional romance narrative.

24. *Margaret Mitchell's "Gone with the Wind" Letters*, 102.

25. Ibid., 38.

26. Ibid., 37–40.

27. Ibid., 126–27.

28. Ibid., 38.

29. Ibid., 1034–37.

30. Ibid., 111.

31. Ibid., 108–11.

32. Ibid., 19–21.

33. Ibid., 73–75.

34. Herschel Brickell, New York *Evening Post*, 22 October 1936. The column is reprinted in part in *Margaret Mitchell's "Gone with the Wind" Letters*, 80.

35. See, for example, Madonne M. Miner's "Guaranteed to Please: Twentieth-Century American Women's Bestsellers," *Gender and Reading: Essays on Readers, Texts, and Contexts*, ed. Elizabeth Flynn and Patrocinio Schweickart (Baltimore: Johns Hopkins University Press, 1986), which explores *Gone with the Wind* as a text preoccupied with "improvident mothers, hungry daughters, and empty houses" (193–200). Janice Radway in her *Reading the Romance: Women, Patriarchy, and Popular Literature* (Chapel Hill: University of North Carolina Press, 1984) provides a study and analysis of why women find the reading of popular romance to be a means by which they may reconcile changing attitudes of gender behavior at the end of the twentieth century with more traditional modes of social behavior.

36. *Margaret Mitchell's "Gone with the Wind" Letters*, 80–82.

37. *Margaret Mitchell's "Gone with the Wind" Letters*, 111.

38. Ibid., 337.

39. Ibid., 238.

40. Ibid., 22.

41. Ibid., 5.

42. Ibid., 119, 142.

43. John Marsh's letter to Herschel Brickell is quoted in part in Farr (and Stephens Mitchell), *Margaret Mitchell of Atlanta*, 153.

44. Stephens Mitchell's reaction to Marsh's "extraordinary" response is recorded in Farr (and Stephens Mitchell), *Margaret Mitchell of Atlanta*, 153–54.

45. Mitchell's letter to Herschel Brickell concerning her fear of her husband's reaction is published in part in Farr (and Stephens Mitchell), *Margaret Mitchell of Atlanta*, 155–56. In Richard Harwell's editing of *Margaret Mitchell's "Gone with the Wind" Letters* certain portions of Mitchell's highly wrought and emotionally expressed reaction to her fame and her fears for her husband are deleted from the published text.

46. Ibid., 15.
47. Ibid., 81.
48. Ibid., 108–11.

Chapter Five

1. Unpublished manuscript quoted by Joseph Blotner in his *Faulkner: A Biography,* vol. 1 (New York: Random House, 1974), 811.
2. The best sources to the intellectual conflicts within southern modernism are Daniel Joseph Singal's *The War Within: From Victorian to Modernist Thought in the South, 1919–1945* (Chapel Hill: University of North Carolina Press, 1982), especially the chapters "Howard W. Odum and Social Science in the South" (115–52) and "The Agrarian Response to Modernism" (198–231), and Fred Hobson's *Tell about the South: The Southern Rage to Explain* (Baton Rouge: Louisiana State University Press, 1983), especially chapter 3, "Odum, Davidson, and the Sociological Proteus" (180–243).
3. The most important southern writers in the mid-1930s were Erskine Caldwell, Caroline Miller, James Branch Cabell, and Thomas Wolfe.
4. See Woodward, "The Search for Southern Identity," in *The Burden of Southern History.* See also his "The Irony of Southern History," in *Southern Renascence: The Literature of the Modern South,* ed. Louis D. Rubin, Jr., and Robert D. Jacobs (Baltimore: Johns Hopkins University Press, 1953). Also, note Hobson's *Tell about the South,* 3–16.
5. See Louis D. Rubin's "Trouble in the Land" in his *A Gallery of Southerners* (Baton Rouge: Louisiana State University Press, 1982), especially 172–73.
6. William Faulkner, *Absalom, Absalom!* (New York: Random House, 1936), 9.
7. Malcolm Cowley, *The Faulkner-Cowley File Letters and Memories, 1944–1962* (New York: Viking, 1966), 25.
8. The quotation is derived from an unpublished Faulkner manuscript cited in Blotner's *Faulkner: A Biography,* 811.
9. These developments are discussed in detail in Gaston, *The New South Creed*; Hobson, *Tell about the South*; Richard Gray, *The Literature of Memory: Modern Writers of the South* (Baltimore: Johns Hopkins University Press, 1977), and Richard King, *A Southern Renaissance: The Cultural Awakening of the American South, 1930–1955* (New York: Oxford University Press, 1980).
10. Faulkner, *Absalom, Absalom!,* 261–262.
11. Unpublished Faulkner manuscript, Blotner's *Faulkner: A Biography,* 811.
12. Rubin, "Scarlett O'Hara and the Two Quentin Compsons," *A Gallery of Southerners,* 26–48.
13. See Farr (and Stephens Mitchell), *Margaret Mitchell of Atlanta,* for a

copy of Professor Charles Everett's report on the novel to Macmillan Publishing Co. Everett, a professor in the English Department of Columbia University, suggested that Mitchell "strengthen the last page" by providing a clearer conclusion (97–102).

14. Rubin, "Scarlett O'Hara and the Two Quentin Compsons," 28.

15. For Mitchell's comments about Faulkner and a copy of some of the contents of her own letter to Faulkner, see *Margaret Mitchell's "Gone with the Wind" Letters,* 88–89, 421.

16. See Gray's *The Literature of Memory* for a clear discussion of the social and historical context of southern literary modernism (1–39). Gray does not consider the text of *Gone with the Wind* in any detail; in fact, he seems to confuse the novel with the film, for he refers to the book's "plantation legend" that "lapses into a kind of easy nostalgia" (93, 107). Mitchell chose to place her novel in the North Georgia setting of Clayton County on a working farm far removed from the plantation legends of coastal Georgia and South Carolina, and she wrote "about war and hard times in Georgia" (*Margaret Mitchell's "Gone with the Wind" Letters,* 1), which she did not believe to be a subject of "easy nostalgia." The film version of her text, over which she had no artistic control, did romanticize and simplify the text of the novel in the manner Gray refers to.

17. Frederick L. Gwynn and Joseph L. Blotner, eds., *Faulkner in the University: Class Conferences at the University of Virginia, 1957–1958* (Charlottesville: University of Virginia Press, 1959), 273–74.

18. Faulkner, *Absalom, Absalom!,* 127.

19. Gwynn and Blotner, eds., *Faulkner in the University,* 48–49.

20. Ibid., 73.

21. An excellent exploration of Faulkner's use of Gothic elements in *Absalom, Absalom!* is included in Michael Millgate's *The Achievement of William Faulkner* (New York: Random House, 1966), 150–64.

22. For recent studies of Faulkner's creation of female characters, see *Faulkner and Women: Faulkner and Yoknapatawpha,* ed. Doreen Fowler and Ann J. Abadie (Jackson: University Press of Mississippi, 1986).

23. *Margaret Mitchell's "Gone with the Wind Letters,"* 65.

24. William Faulkner in Malcolm Cowley, ed., *Writers at Work: The "Paris Review" Interviews* (New York: Viking, 1958), 141.

25. Allen Tate, *The Fathers* (New York: Putnam's, 1938), 22.

26. See Gray's "The Nashville Agrarians" in his *Literature of Memory* for a lucid discussion of the relation between Allen Tate's poetry and his single novel.

27. Tate, *The Fathers,* 22.

28. Ibid., 43–44.

29. Ibid., 179–80.

30. Ibid., 186–87.

31. Ibid., 11–12.
32. See Ruth Vande Kieft's *Eudora Welty* (New York: Twayne, 1962), Alfred Appel, Jr.'s *A Season of Dreams: The Fiction of Eudora Welty* (Baton Rouge: Louisiana State University Press, 1965), Michael Kreyling's *Eudora Welty's Achievement of Order* (Baton Rouge: Louisiana State University Press, 1980), and Elizabeth Even's *Eudora Welty* (New York: Unger, 1981) for biographical and critical commentary of Welty's work and art.
33. Eudora Welty, *Delta Wedding* (New York: Harcourt Brace, 1946), 3–4.
34. See Charles T. Bunting's "'The Interior World': An Interview with Eudora Welty," *Southern Review* 8 (October 1972): 711–35.
35. *Margaret Mitchell's "Gone with the Wind" Letters,* 115.
36. Eudora Welty, "Place in Fiction," *Three Papers on Fiction* (New York: Harcourt Brace, 1957), 11.

Chapter Six

1. *Margaret Mitchell's "Gone with the Wind" Letters,* 95.
2. Ibid., 247–48.
3. Ibid., 247–48.
4. Farr (and Stephens Mitchell), *Margaret Mitchell of Atlanta,* 121.
5. Ibid., 121–23.
6. Ibid., 145.
7. Ibid., 147.
8. *Margaret Mitchell's "Gone with the Wind" Letters,* 225–28.
9. Farr (and Stephens Mitchell), *Margaret Mitchell of Atlanta,* 156–57.
10. Ibid., 158.
11. Ibid., 140.
12. Ibid., 144.
13. Ibid., 161.
14. Margaret Mitchell and her husband are quoted in Harold Martin's "Atlanta's Most Brilliant Event," *"Gone with the Wind" As Book and Film,* compiled and edited by Richard Harwell (Columbia: University of South Carolina, 1983), 148–50.
15. Thomas Dixon, Jr., *The Clansman* (New York: Doubleday, Page, 1905), 149.
16. The most useful sources to the history of American filmmaking, especially with regard to the Griffith and Selznick Civil War films, are Robert M. Henderson's *D. W. Griffith: His Life and Work* (New York: Oxford University Press, 1972), Thomas Cripps's *Slow Fade to Black: The Negro in American Film, 1900–1942* (New York: Oxford University Press, 1977), and David Thomson's *America in the Dark: Hollywood and the Gift of Unreality* (New York: Morrow, 1977). Several popular treatments of the making of *Gone with the*

Wind are Gavin Lambert's *GWTW: The Making of "Gone with the Wind"* (Boston: Little Brown, 1973) and Roland Flamini's *Scarlett, Rhett, and a Cast of Thousands: The Filming of "Gone with the Wind"* (New York: Macmillan, 1975).

17. David Selznick to Sidney Howard, 6 January 1937, *Memo from David Selznick,* ed. Rudy Behlmer (New York: Viking, 1972), 151.

18. See the fine article by Thomas Cripps, "Winds and Change: *Gone with the Wind* and Racism as a National Issue," in *Recasting: "Gone with the Wind" in American Culture,* ed. Darden Asbury Pyron (Miami: University Presses of Florida, 1983), 137–52.

19. For an excellent study of how white men linked the vulnerability of women with the behavior of black males, see Jacquelyn D. Hull's *Revolt against Chivalry* (New York: Columbia University Press, 1979), 153.

20. Selznick to Howard, 6 January 1937, *Memo from David Selznick,* 151.

21. See Thomson's *America in the Dark,* 37–39, for a lucid discussion of how film makers sought to idealize their subject matters on film.

22. See Edward Campbell's *The Celluloid South: Hollywood and the Southern Myth* (Knoxville: University of Tennessee Press, 1981), especially 3–32, for a study of the development of a southern "mythology" in American filmmaking.

23. For an analysis of the development of historically based films, see Robert Sklar's *Movie-Made America: A Social History of American Movies* (New York: Random House, 1975) and Garth Jowett's *Film: The Democratic Art* (Boston: Little, Brown, 1976).

24. The poll was reported in the *New York Times,* 20 December 1939, shortly after the film's premiere in Atlanta on 15 December 1939.

25. Campbell, *The Celluloid South,* 134–40.

26. *Margaret Mitchell's "Gone with the Wind" Letters,* 249–53.

27. Ibid., 252.

28. Ibid., 260–63.

29. Ibid., 263.

30. Ibid., 267–69.

31. Ibid., 357–59.

32. Farr (and Stephens Mitchell), *Margaret Mitchell of Atlanta,* 198–201.

33. Ibid., 209–10.

34. Ibid., 210–18.

Chapter Seven

1. *Margaret Mitchell of Atlanta,* 229.

2. Allen Tate, "Ode to the Confederate Dead," *Allen Tate: Collected Poems, 1919–1976* (New York: Farrar, Straus & Giroux, 1977), 20–23.

3. *Margaret Mitchell's "Gone with the Wind" Letters,* 230–31.

4. Ibid.
5. Ibid., 183–85.
6. Ibid., 180–82.
7. Farr (and Stephens Mitchell), *Margaret Mitchell of Atlanta,* 225.
8. Farr (and Stephens Mitchell), *Margaret Mitchell of Atlanta,* 229.

Selected Bibliography

PRIMARY WORK

Gone with the Wind. New York: Macmillan, 1936.

SECONDARY WORKS

Appel, Alfred, Jr. *A Season of Dreams: The Fiction of Eudora Welty.* Baton Rouge: Louisiana State University Press, 1965.

Appleby, Joyce. "Reconciliation and the Northern Novelist, 1865–1880." *Civil War History* 10 (June 1964): 117–29.

Bartley, Numan. *The Creation of Modern Georgia.* Athens: University of Georgia Press, 1983. The most thorough source on the history and development of Georgia.

Baym, Nina. *Women's Fiction: A Guide to Novels by and about Women, 1820–1870.* Ithaca, N.Y.: Cornell University Press, 1978.

Behlmer, Rudy, ed. *Memo from David Selznick.* New York: Viking, 1972.

Bell, Malcolm, Jr. *Major Butler's Legacy: Five Generations of a Slave-Holding Family.* Athens: University of Georgia Press, 1987.

Blotner, Joseph. *Faulkner: A Biography.* New York: Random House, 1974.

Bunting, Charles. "'The Interior World': An Interview with Eudora Welty." *Southern Review* 8 (October 1972): 711–35.

Campbell, Edward. *The Celluloid South: Hollywood and Southern Myth.* Knoxville: University of Tennessee Press, 1981. Provides useful information and insight into the creation of the film *Gone with the Wind.*

Cawalti, John G. *Adventure, Mystery, and Romance: Formula Stories as Art and Popular Culture.* Chicago: University of Chicago Press, 1976.

Cott, Nancy. *The Bonds of Womanhood.* New Haven, Conn.: Yale University Press, 1977.

Cowley, Malcolm. *The Faulkner-Cowley File: Letters and Memories.* New York: Viking, 1966.

———. *Writers at Work: The "Paris Review" Interviews.* New York: Viking, 1958.

Cripps, Thomas. "Winds of Change." In *"Gone with the Wind" in American Culture,* edited by Darden Asbury Pyron, pp. 137–52. Miami: University of Florida Press, 1983.

Crozier, Alice. *The Novels of Harriet Beecher Stowe*. New York: Oxford University Press, 1969.

Dittmer, John. *Black Georgia in the Progressive Era, 1900–1920*. Urbana: University of Illinois Press, 1977.

Dixon, Thomas. *The Clansman*. New York: Doubleday, Page, 1905.

Douglas, Ann. *The Feminization of American Culture*. New York: Knopf, 1977.

Edwards, Anne. *The Road to Tara: The Life of Margaret Mitchell*. New York: Dell, 1983. Edwards's treatment of Mitchell's life is a popularized version; little attention is paid to Mitchell's writings.

Even, Elizabeth. *Eudora Welty*. New York: Unger, 1981.

Farr, Finis (and Stephens Mitchell). *Margaret Mitchell of Atlanta: The author of "Gone with the Wind."* New York: Morrow, 1965. Authorized biography with excerpts of the unpublished memoir of Stephens Mitchell, unpublished family correspondence, and other family sources of information. It does not provide critical evaluation of Mitchell's writings.

Faulkner, William. *Absalom, Absalom!* New York: Random House, 1936.

Fisher, Philip. *Hard Facts: Setting and Form in the American Novel*. New York: Oxford University Press, 1985.

Fishkin, Shelley Fisher. *From Fact into Fiction: Journalism and Imaginative Writing in America*. Baltimore: Johns Hopkins University Press, 1985.

Flamini, Roland. *Scarlett, Rhett, and a Cast of Thousands: The Filming of "Gone with the Wind"*. New York: Macmillan, 1975. Amusing, pictorial treatment of the creation of the film *Gone with the Wind*.

Fowler, Foreen, and Ann Abadie, eds. *Faulkner and Women*. Jackson: University of Mississippi Press, 1986.

Gaston, Paul. *The New South Creed*. New York: Knopf, 1970.

Geary, Susan. "The Domestic Novel as a Commercial Commodity." Bibliographical Society of America, July 1976, 369–70.

Gelfant, Blanche. *Women Writing in America: Voices in Collage*. Hanover, N.H.: University Press of New England, 1984.

Gray, Richard. *The Literature of Memory: Modern Writers of the American South*. Baltimore: Johns Hopkins University Press, 1977.

———. *Writing the South*. Baltimore: Johns Hopkins University Press, 1986.

Gwynn, Frederick, and Joseph Blotner, eds. *Faulkner in the University*. Charlottesville: University of Virginia Press, 1959.

Harwell, Richard, ed. *"Gone with the Wind" as Book and Film*. Columbia: University of South Carolina Press, 1983. Collection of sources for the study of the novel and the film version of *Gone with the Wind*, key newspaper accounts of and by Mitchell, book reviews of the novel, articles related to the film, and reprintings of several recent scholarly articles about the novel by Floyd Watkins, Henry Steele Commager, and Leslie Fiedler.

———, ed. *Margaret Mitchell's "Gone with the Wind" Letters, 1936–1949*. New

York: Macmillan, 1976. Best-selling selection of Mitchell's correspondence after the publication of *Gone with the Wind*. Some important letters
are not reprinted with full text, and Harwell offers almost no information
about the complexity of Mitchell's letter-writing self or about the range
of letter writers who sought her replies.

Henderson, Robert. *M. D. W. Griffith: His Life and Work*. New York: Oxford
University Press, 1972.

Hobson, Fred. *Tell about the South: The Southern Rage to Explain*. Baton Rouge:
Louisiana State University Press, 1983.

Horowitz, Helen. *Alma Mater: Design and Experience in Women's Colleges*. New
York: Knopf, 1984.

Hull, Jacquelyn. *Revolt against Chivalry*. New York: Columbia University
Press, 1979.

Hunter, Floyd. *Community Power Structures: A Study of Decision Makers*. Chapel
Hill: University of North Carolina Press, 1953.

————. *Community Power Succession: Atlanta's Policy Makers Revisited*. Chapel
Hill: University of North Carolina Press, 1980.

Jones, Anne Godwyn. *Tomorrow Is Another Day: The Woman Writer in the South,
1859–1936*. Baton Rouge: Louisiana State University Press, 1981. Useful source for southern women's writings, especially about the Civil War;
Mitchell receives treatment in the final chapter.

Jones, M. W. "Me and My Book." *Georgia Review* 16 (Summer 1962): 180–
87.

Jowart, Garth. *Film: A Democratic Art*. Boston: Little, Brown, 1976.

Juergens, George. *Joseph Pulitzer and the New York World*. Princeton: Princeton
University Press, 1966.

Kelley, Mary. *Private Woman, Public Stage*. New York: Oxford University
Press, 1984.

King, Richard. *A Southern Renaissance*. New York: Oxford University Press,
1980.

Kreyling, Michael. *Eudora Welty's Achievement of Order*. Baton Rouge: Louisiana
State University Press, 1980.

Lambert, Gavin. *GWTW: The Making of "Gone with the Wind."* Boston: Little,
Brown, 1973. Study of the making of the film version and of the film
as a work of American popular culture in the 1930s.

Lukács, György. *The Historical Novel*, translated by Hannah and Stanley
Mitchell. Boston: Beacon, 1962.

Millgate, Michael. *The Achievement of William Faulkner*. New York: Random
House, 1966.

Mussell, Kay. *Women's Gothic and Romantic Fiction*. Westport, Conn.: Greenwood, 1981.

O'Brien, Michael. *The Idea of the American South, 1920–1941*. Baltimore:
Johns Hopkins University Press, 1979.

————. *Rethinking the South*. Baltimore: Johns Hopkins University Press, 1988.

O'Neill, William. *Divorce in the Progressive Era*. New Haven, Conn.: Yale University Press, 1967.

Osterweiss, Rollin. *The Myth of the Lost Cause, 1865–1900*. Hamden, Conn.: Archon, 1973.

Pyron, Darden Asbury. *Recasting: "Gone with the Wind" in American Culture*. Miami: University of Florida Press, 1983. Collection reprints several important essays by Louis Rubin, Malcolm Cowley, Anne Jones, and Thomas Cripps.

Radway, Janet. *Reading the Romance: Women, Patriarchy, and Popular Culture*. Chapel Hill: University of North Carolina Press, 1984.

Range, Willard. *A Century of Georgia Agriculture*. Athens: University of Georgia Press, 1984.

Rubin, Louis D., Jr. *A Gallery of Southerners*. Baton Rouge: Louisiana State University Press, 1982. Study explores *Gone with the Wind* in the context of other southern literary masters of fiction.

————, ed. *A History of Southern Literature*. Baton Rouge: Louisiana State University Press, 1985.

Schudson, Michael. *Discovering the News: A Social History of American Newspapers*. New York: Basic, 1978.

Scott, Anne Firor. *The Southern Lady: From Pedestal to Politics, 1830–1930*. Chicago: University of Chicago Press, 1970.

Singal, Daniel Joseph. *The War Within: From Victorian to Modernist Thought in the South, 1919–1945*. Chapel Hill: University of North Carolina Press, 1982. Intellectual history of the period of Mitchell's development as a writer in the South.

Sklar, Robert. *Movie-Made America: A Social History of the American Film*. New York: Random House, 1975.

Smith-Rosenberg, Carroll. *Disorderly Conduct: Vision of Gender in Victorian America*. New York: Knopf, 1985. Essays by Smith-Rosenberg that develop her theses concerning a separate sphere or "female world" that codified relations between women in the nineteenth-century American South and continued during the Progressive era.

————. "The Secret World of Love and Ritual: Relations between Women in Nineteenth-Century America." *Signs* 1, no. 1 (Autumn 1975): 1–29.

Soltow, Lee. *Men and Work in the United States, 1850–1870*. New Haven, Conn.: Yale University Press, 1975.

Stowe, Harriet Beecher. *Uncle Tom's Cabin*, edited by Kenneth Lynn. Cambridge: Harvard University Press, 1962.

Swanberg, W. A. *Citizen Hearst*. New York: Scribner's, 1961.

Tate, Allen. *Collected Poems, 1919–1976*. New York: Farrar, Straus & Giroux, 1977.

————. *The Fathers*. New York: Putnam's, 1938.

Thomson, David. *America in the Dark: Hollywood and the Gift of Unreality*. New York: Morrow, 1977.

Tompkins, Jane. *Sensational Designs: The Cultural Work of American Fiction, 1790–1860*. New York: Oxford University Press, 1985.

Vande Kieft, Ruth. *Eudora Welty*. New York: Twayne, 1962.

Watkins, Floyd. *"Gone with the Wind* as Vulgar Literature." *Southern Literary Journal* 2 (Spring 1970): 86–103.

Welty, Eudora. *Delta Wedding*. New York: Harcourt, 1946.

————. *Three Papers on Fiction*. New York: Harcourt, 1957.

Wilson, Charles R. *Baptized in Blood: The Religion of the Lost Cause, 1865–1920*. Athens: University of Georgia Press, 1980.

Wilson, Edmund. *Patriotic Gore*. New York: Oxford, 1962.

Woodward, C. Vann. *The Burden of Southern History*. Baton Rouge: Louisiana State University Press, 1960.

Wyatt-Brown, Bertram. *Southern Honor: Ethics and Behavior in the Old South*. New York: Oxford University Press, 1982. Critical analysis of the ethical and philosophical significance of southern behavior, especially toward women. Mitchell's imaginative terrain in *Gone with the Wind* is explored from the point of view of history and sociology.

Index